THE SEARCH FOR FREEDOM

The Search for Freedom

*Demolishing the Strongholds that Diminish
Your Faith, Hope, and Confidence in God*

Robert S. McGee

Servant Publications
Ann Arbor, Michigan

Vine Books is an imprint of Servant Publications especially designed to serve evangelical Christians.

Scripture quotations, unless otherwise noted, are from *The Holy Bible: New International Version* (NIV), © 1973, 1978, 1984 International Bible Society. Used by permission of Zondervan Bible Publishers.

Selected Scripture quotations are from the New American Standard Bible (NAS), © 1960, 1962, 1963, 1968, 1971, 1972, 1973, 1975, 1977 by the Lockman Foundation. All rights reserved. Used by permission.

The names and characterizations in this book that are drawn from the author's counseling and personal experience are rendered pseudonymously and as fictional composites. Any similarity between the names and characterizations of these individuals and real people is unintended and purely coincidental.

Published by Servant Publications
P.O. Box 8617
Ann Arbor, Michigan 48107

Cover photograph © The Stock Market/Tom Stewart, 1993
Cover design by Multnomah Graphics

95 96 97 98 99 10 9 8 7 6 5 4 3 2 1

Printed in the United States of America
ISBN 0-89283-862-0

Library of Congress Cataloging-in-Publication Data

McGee, Robert S.
    The search for freedom : demolishing the strongholds that diminish your faith, hope, and confidence in God / Robert S. McGee.
        p.   cm.
    SBN 0-89283-862-0
    1. Freedom (Theology)   2. Mental health—Religious aspects—Christianity.
I. Title
BT810.2.M38   1995
241'.4—dc20   94-45757
                                                        CIP

Contents

Acknowledgments

My deepest gratitude to these friends and co-workers who offered invaluable help, insight, and inspiration.

Stan	Kevin
Guy	Sandy
Janice	Stuart
Tom	Don
Larry	Shannon
Liz	Taylor
Dave	Melanie
Jennifer	Wayne
Marilyn	LaDean
Rujon	Steve
Phocion	

How to Use This Book

Those of you who know me and have read my books will recognize this verse, "You shall know the truth and the truth shall make you free" (John 8:32), which is the foundation of my ministry. Jesus is referring, I believe, to the truths of who we are in Christ as well as to the truths about Satan and how he has deceived us. I wrote this book to help you understand more clearly how Satan may have gained a stronghold in your life. This stronghold may be keeping you from experiencing the freedom that God longs for you to experience.

It's one thing to read a book and to feel that the information is helpful and insightful. It's something altogether different to apply information to your life and to change your behavior. In order to help you do that, I've included a list of questions at the end of each chapter. If you truly want to be free, I strongly encourage you to take the time to work through these sections before moving on to the next chapter. As you reflect on each question, pray that God will give you the courage and insight to honestly answer it. Be persistent in this. With God's help, there is no reason why you cannot be free... but you must seek his help and obey his voice.

Because these questions were written for individuals, those included at the end of each chapter may not be suitable for group discussion. With this in mind, I included a list of questions in the back of the book that could be used in groups. If you are reading this book as part of a group study, don't assume you can skip the questions at the end of each chapter. If you really want to benefit from this book, you need to take time to honestly answer these questions first, then move on to those for the group. Yes, this will take some time... perhaps quite a bit of time. But isn't your freedom worth that?

It is my prayer that God will use this book to "enlighten the eyes of your heart."

Sincerely,

Robert S. McGee

Robert S. McGee

CHAPTER 1

How Freedom Is Lost

A lmost everyone I talk to expresses a strong desire for a greater sense of freedom in life. I believe God is responsible for that desire, and he lets us know such freedom is possible. Jesus himself promised, "You will know the truth, and the truth will set you free" (Jn 8:32).

Yet look around. Do you know many people who say they feel truly free? I don't. Most of us are on a search for freedom. We believe that freedom is a reasonable and achievable goal, yet we never quite seem to accomplish it. We often go through our entire lives in bondage to one thing or another in an ever-elusive quest to break free. Some give up the search after a while. Others of us try to convince ourselves that we are free when we actually aren't. But if we conduct a search for freedom on our own—without God's help—we will accomplish the opposite of what we hope to achieve, as Susie did.

At eighteen, Susie was a vivacious young girl with a strong desire to be free. To her, that meant becoming independent of her parents, whom she felt did not allow her to take adequate responsibility for her own life. Their overprotective tendencies did not provide her the total freedom she sought.

Today, at twenty-one, Susie has two small children who need continual attention amid their frequent bouts of crying and screaming. On top of these responsibilities, Susie is expected to keep the house clean, do the shopping, run errands, and do all those other things associated with motherhood. In addition, her husband's expectations for her seem unending. She is trying so hard to be a good wife and mother that she has almost forgotten how to be herself. In any spare moments during her hectic day, she dreams about those carefree days when her only major problem in life was two loving parents who were a bit overprotective. Susie thought she was breaking free. But her search for freedom only led to further complications and obligations.

If we conduct a search for freedom on our own—without God's help—we will accomplish the opposite of what we hope to achieve.

Paul's life tells a similar story. Paul had been a product of the sixties. He and his friends knew the secret to a satisfying life: "Don't pay attention to those stifling mores of the plastic generation. Oh, sure, you have to go through the motions and look just right. Get a law degree from one of the prestigious universities. Marry an attractive woman. Create a network of the right kinds of friends—friends with power. On the outside, look like the establishment. But give yourself permission to enjoy the wilder side of life." To Paul that meant becoming intimate with the wife of a powerful politician. As the lawyer for the couple, it also meant arranging shady deals and covering them up.

Now, however, everything was coming undone. He had been found out. Before long, everyone would know all his secrets. After years of "freedom" when he felt untouchable and above the law, he could no longer avoid the truth. He felt trapped. He couldn't live without the perks of power and wealth, or so he thought. And the loss of prestige was too much to give up. The spectacle of his impending shame would be too painful to bear.

As he thought about these things, Paul held a .38 calibre revolver in his hands. In a few minutes, he planned to end a life that had been as full as he could possibly make it but was still empty. As he saw it, death was the only remaining option for freedom.

As you think back across your life, you can probably list a number of Susies and Pauls you know personally. People all around you are searching, struggling to be free. Perhaps your own name is on that list as someone wanting desperately to be free, only to find yourself more deeply enslaved with every effort.

FREEDOM COME, FREEDOM GO

So what *is* freedom? I believe it is escaping the grasp of anything that desires to capture and enslave. But the problem is that the harder we struggle to become free, the more freedom we seem to lose.

How can we explain this dilemma? I think we must be very careful as we determine where to find freedom and how to go about achieving it. Susie tried to find freedom in a new relationship with a young man only to become controlled by him. Paul tried to find freedom by experiencing whatever lust and power he could, and it consumed him.

Others we know have tried to find freedom from loneliness through the experience of marriage, only to be married and lonely. Some have tried to succeed in finding freedom from a sense of inferiority only to find success hard to handle when you feel so inferior.

With one exception—Jesus, who is the truth that sets us free—everything we flee to in hope of finding refuge and freedom has the potential to enslave us. Even those of us who are fiercely independent and rely only on our own abilities can get caught up in a driven performance orientation that never allows us a taste of rest and freedom.

Many of us know about this all too well. Our choices turn into compulsions. Our search for freedom results in less freedom than ever before. Caught in a web of our own making, we struggle against forces we do not understand. Every effort seems to make us more entwined, with less energy to fight. Hope escapes us like so much sand slipping through our fingers.

Questions without answers begin to flood our minds. What are we trying to gain freedom from? Why do we find ourselves so caught when we've tried so hard too be free? Is there something intrinsically wrong with us?

A TRULY FALLEN AND SINFUL MAN

A man recently walked into my office. He had a vile beginning to his life. As a child, he could accurately be described as sinful. I know this sounds like a harsh description, but my source is totally reliable. He had developed an evil conscience yet was unaware of this fact. His life was corrupt and deceitful, full of rebellion. His thoughts were evil and lustful. Because of his heritage, it is said he was dominated by Satan.

What could I do to help this man? Try as I might, I could do nothing. *For I was that man.*

Now, I don't like to think of myself as depraved, corrupt, or deceitful. If asked to give three words to describe myself, those aren't the ones I would begin with. Yet if I understand the truth of Scripture, those might be some of the words God would use to describe my fleshly nature. Some of the clearest truths of Scripture have to do with the effects of humanity's fall and how our lives are still affected. These truths, however, are also some of the least appreciated. Let's look at just a few of these truths to get a clearer picture of what fallen humanity is.

We are sinful: "You were dead in your transgressions and sins, in which you used to live when you followed the ways of this world and of the ruler of the kingdom of the air, the spirit who is now at work in those who are disobedient. All of us also lived among them at one time, gratifying the cravings of our sinful nature and following its desires and thoughts. Like the rest, we were by nature objects of wrath" (Eph 2:1-3).

As bad as this description may sound, we cannot overlook the truth of what it is saying. We also need to understand that this was the condition of our minds as we developed our patterns of thought and action. We don't normally consider them evil, yet many of these patterns that were developed by the flesh when we were young may be responsible for most of our struggles today.

We are ignorant, blind, and with darkened understanding. "They are darkened in their understanding and separated from the life of God because of the ignorance that is in them due to the hardening of their hearts" (Eph 4:18).

What does it mean to have a darkened understanding? A mind that develops its understanding of life apart from God is darkened. Obviously, a darkened mind will produce a corresponding darkened understanding of life, and this was exactly the state of our minds as we developed our understanding of life as children. Is it any wonder that we can carry such tremendous deception without knowing it?

The rest of this verse points out our fallen ignorance. Being ignorant is bad enough. But not understanding that we created our basic beliefs about life during childhood ignorance can be devastating. It's doubly tragic to be ignorant about one's ignorance.

We are evil in conscience. "Let us draw near to God with a sincere heart in full assurance of faith, having our hearts sprinkled to cleanse us from a guilty [evil] conscience and having our bodies washed with pure water" (Heb 10:22). Genesis 6:5 also tells us, "The Lord saw how great man's wickedness on the earth had become, and that every inclination of the thoughts of his heart was only evil all the time."

Perhaps no phrase better describes our culture than "evil conscience." What was once universally accepted as wrong is now looked on as right, and those who still hold to the original understanding of right are considered wrong. Tolerance is now considered the highest virtue. Speaking against immoral behavior is considered bordering on a hate crime. But as we consider the moral insanity that runs rampant in the world this very minute, realize that this only reflects what was learned during the early formative years of life. You've probably seen children who get angry and would do a lot of damage if they were able to do so. Those who become adults without changing those patterns are able to do a lot of damage.

We have corrupt and deceitful hearts. "The heart is deceitful above all things and beyond cure. Who can understand it?" (Jer 17:9).

How can something that feels so right be so wrong? When our thoughts are distorted, our emotions reflect the quality of those thoughts. Many times our hearts are deceitful because they are first deceived. But because of our darkened understanding, we don't realize our hearts are deceived. If I asked you to list ten things you are deceived about, you couldn't do it. The very nature of being deceived is that the deception goes unnoticed.

We have desperately sick hearts. Not only are our hearts deceitful, they are also desperately sick—as Jeremiah says, "beyond cure." Sickness indicates abnormality, that they are not functioning as designed and intended. The heart has been poisoned with fleshly and destructive input since birth. No wonder it is sick!

The question asked in Jeremiah 17:9, "Who can understand it?" has an implied answer: no one can. No one, that is, except God himself. This is why it makes no sense to try to correct the human condition using only human wisdom.

We are in obstinate rebellion. "The sinful mind is hostile to God. It does not submit to God's law, nor can it do so" (Rom 8:7).

A mind hostile toward God is not inclined to do things God's way. If I bought a car and did everything the manufacturer said *not* to do, I shouldn't be surprised when the car stops functioning well or even breaks down altogether. If we live our lives in opposition to the things God says to do, should it surprise us that we struggle so much?

I urge you to dwell on this issue of natural human depravity until you are convinced that you need to reevaluate whatever fleshly "wisdom" you may have accumulated to this point. Here are just a few more verses and characteristics to consider before moving on.

In our fleshly state, we are:

> Children of disobedience ....Ephesians 2:2
> Hard of heart.............................Ephesians 4:18
> Lustful and ungodly...............................Jude 18
> Dominated by Satan.........................Acts 26:18
> Servants of sin ....Romans 6:16-18

DO WE KNOW OUR TRUE CONDITION?

The previous passages are not only God's assessment of my condition at birth but also his description of *your* condition at birth as well. Why do these descriptions seem to be at such variance with our perceptions of ourselves?

I think most people have two major misconceptions. The first is suggested in Jesus' statement, "Anyone who looks at a woman lustfully has already committed adultery with her in his heart" (Mt 5:28). Here Jesus clarifies an important point: our true condition is not necessarily what we believe it to be. We have a tendency to think we're superior to others because we don't display certain forms of wickedness in our external behavior. But that is a deception which leaves us with a truly distorted understanding of our spiritual condition.

These days, it's not popular to speak or write about the depravity of humankind. Few Christians give the matter adequate thought. They know some of the verses previously quoted, but they don't seem to take them seriously or let their truth sink in. Even at salvation, most people have only an inkling of the true state of their condition. Determining "goodness" remains a matter of comparing one's external behavior to the external behavior of others.

We do not understand the true nature of the flesh. (Throughout this book I will use the term *flesh* to refer to the natural part of ourselves, as distinguished from our spiritual selves.) We can never find freedom without coming to grips with the fallen nature of our flesh. The flesh is not redeemed at salvation; it remains fallen and victimized by sin. We may learn to avoid corrupt external behavior, but the nature of the flesh does not change. *We are born in sin and we struggle against a fallen nature throughout our lifetimes.* I cannot emphasize this point too strongly. Until you understand your fleshly nature, your search for freedom will be hindered.

For example, a woman came to me for counseling many years ago. Her husband had been caught in an adulterous affair. The woman was justifiably angry in the beginning. But she came to me several years after her husband's infidelity, and she was still filled with rage. After a period of counseling, I got tired of hearing what a worthless slug this guy was. I wasn't sure this woman believed she was just as capable of making a similar mistake based on her own sinful nature. So I asked her, "Don't you think you could easily do the same thing?"

I thought she was going to come unglued. She protested that such a thing was impossible. She said that kind of behavior was below her. Then I asked her if it would be OK for me to pray that the Holy Spirit would remove his constraining power in her life so that she could see just how vile her flesh really was. She refused, but in a short time she saw that she was just as depraved as anyone else on earth—including her unfaithful husband. That was the last I heard of how superior she was. And eventually, her acceptance of this truth helped her find freedom from her ongoing pain.

Knowledge of one's own human condition is the key to having compassion for others.

I was recently asked how I "got away with" confronting people about their worst behaviors without them becoming upset with me. I shared that it is because regardless of how corrupt the person's behavior might be I know I am entirely capable of doing worse. I know that only the grace of God as he works in my life can possibly explain why I'm not in a worse condition than I am. People can tell whether or not counselors are aware of this, and they know that knowledge of one's own human condition is the key to having compassion for others.

Think what a difference it would make if more churches were aware of this simple truth. Frequently, it is only after people get a glimpse of their own depravity that they become motivated to go to church. But when they get there, church members too often give the impression that they are somehow superior to those who come in for help and hope. No wonder visitors aren't too impressed. Who can blame them when they don't come back?

Many Christians exalt the depraved nature of the flesh. How many times have you heard comments such as, "Wouldn't it be wonderful if he accepted Christ? He is so talented"? But God's work is not accomplished by the skills of the flesh. Jesus did not recruit his disciples from the elite or the exceptionally skilled. God, in fact, seems to receive great satisfaction in accomplishing mighty results through the most unlikely people. The bottom line is that God deserves the glory for good things that get done. If we understood the sinful nature of the flesh (how often we rely on the flesh instead of on God), we would be surprised and grateful whenever we saw God do anything in our lives. We would discover why we don't witness more of his power than we do.

Truly, our minds are a clear reflection of our souls. Few of us consider our thought life as important as God does. If we did, we would hold much less confidence in our natural abilities, because our flesh is absolutely corrupt. Perhaps this is why we are told, "Work out your salvation with fear and trembling" (Phil 2:12) and that "If you live according to the sinful nature, you will die; but if by the Spirit you put to death the misdeeds of the body, you will live" (Rom 8:13).

WE'D HATE TO ADMIT IT... BUT...

The second misconception about the nature of our flesh is that we can admire what the flesh can do. We *like* some of our fleshly behaviors. We've learned to produce socially acceptable behavior out of our natural selves. But this is a problem because, while the flesh can produce a certain level of acceptable behavior, it is simultaneously planting the seeds for our eventual destruction. Consider Galatians 5:17 (NAS): "The flesh sets its desire against the Spirit, and the Spirit against the flesh; for these are in opposition to one another, so that you may not do the things that you please." Most Christians lose sight of the fact that we are really at war within ourselves—much less in crisis. We would rather remain content by perceiving ourselves as being reasonably competent and moral.

Sally is one example. At age forty-five she is plump and matronly looking. She has a circle of women friends who share their struggles, and she has felt superior to them and particularly critical of those who were experiencing marital problems and divorce. *What a bunch of losers,* she would think to herself. *I made and kept my marriage commitment. It hasn't been easy, but I've done it.*

It wasn't that Sally and George had such a great marriage. In fact, it had become little more than cohabitation after twenty-five years. And Sally was oblivious to the fact that George wanted more. He eventually found it in a young woman he met at work. When George left, it was just too much for Sally to take. All the condemning thoughts she had previously had toward her friends came crashing down on her.

While no one would have described Sally as depraved or corrupt, she still lived her life at a fleshly level. She did what she could to cope with life, and for years she seemed to get away with it. But one day her life imploded like a tall building being destroyed by dynamite. It simply cratered in upon itself.

THE ENEMY WITHIN

This book is about the patterns and behaviors we learn to rely on in response to the crises of life. Many of these were created by our flesh and have become what Scripture calls strongholds. Often we do not see these strongholds as corrupt or destructive. But most of our problems with living and experiencing the freedom Christ died to give us are directly related to our inner strongholds.

The first step toward freedom is the realization that we have an enemy within. This enemy is so subtle that we can hardly detect it, but it is more deadly than a cancerous tumor. Unfortunately, by the time we become aware of it, it has usually robbed us of an important part of life that cannot be reclaimed.

But we can detect and destroy our strongholds before they destroy us. Much of this book will deal with identifying our strongholds because most of us live with these issues for so long that we will not be able or willing to destroy those strongholds

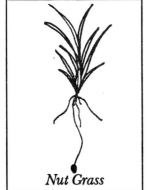

Nut Grass

until we see clearly the evil within our souls. But after we do, we will feel a great sense of urgency that will prepare us for action.

I am convinced that most Christians do not accurately understand the basis of their problems, much less "the way of escape" (see 2 Timothy 2:25-26). Consequently, they end up spasmodically attempting to break free from whatever holds them in its grip, only to be defeated or have yet another problem of equal magnitude arise in its place. Let me explain what I mean.

At one time, I was plagued by nut grass in my yard. Nut grass has nodules on its root system so that if you pull off the top, it will send out two new shoots for the one you ripped off.

My bout with nut grass symbolizes the emotional struggle I've seen in so many people. They only want to deal with the surface manifestations of their problems. For instance, in order to deal with the effects of stress I might work out or zone out (watch TV) or skip out (take a really long vacation). But I have not dealt with why I am struggling with my life. And these methods usual-ly just make the problem worse. By the time most of their problems surface, they have developed much deeper roots that must be dealt with. I'll have more to say about this in later chapters.

Has your search for freedom been like pulling up nut grass? Or have you gotten beyond the surface and struck at some roots? You may have come a long way already and are standing right on the brink of freedom. You know there's more to life than what you've been experiencing, yet the uncertainty of further change is terrifying.

Or maybe you've already attempted an all-out struggle to be free, only to lose the battle. Now, instead of simply feeling that you are in bondage, you feel bound and defeated. Perhaps you feel so weak, exhausted, or hopeless that you've given up and have consigned yourself to a life of bondage, tedium, and control by outside forces you can no longer manage.

Whatever your previous experiences, freedom is possible—for everyone. In fact, if you feel weak and helpless, you may have a head start. No one ever achieves genuine freedom using his or her own power. Any obstacles you face can be overcome, but only through God's power. The sooner we recognize our own inadequacies and turn to God for help to break free, the sooner we will see significant progress.

Freedom, we will discover, is gained by degrees. From my personal experience and all my years of counseling, I am convinced that the search for freedom is almost always a long and difficult process. Paul often chronicled his own struggles, as in Philippians 3:13-14 (NAS): "Brethren, I do not regard myself as having laid hold of it yet; but one thing I do; forgetting what lies behind and reaching forward to what lies ahead, I press on toward the goal for the prize of the upward call of God in Christ Jesus." The results are certainly worth the effort.

Perhaps you've run into the existential theology promoted by certain teachers of most doctrinal persuasions. They suggest that an *experience* is what sets you free from anything and everything.

They say that in the intellectual knowing of truth, complete freedom is gained. They teach that relating to yourself as though you don't really exist is "the way" to recovery. The common thread among all these teachings is that our faith is simple and can be mastered quickly. I certainly haven't found this to be true, and you may come to the same conclusion. Although this philosophy sounds reasonable and hopeful, hundreds of thousands of disillusioned Christians are simply going through the motions of "faith," eventually leaving the church exhibiting little of God's power. They assume that they have tried to live God's way, only to fail.

Although salvation is a complete and instantaneous act of God, we may have to peel off the layers as God initiates healing. As the author of Hebrews 12:1 (NAS) explains, we are to "lay aside any encumbrances."

The choice before us is to continue to be enslaved by all that our natural lives succumb to or to begin our search for freedom. It is my goal to first reveal the pervasiveness of the evil that robs us of the "life... to the full" (Jn 10:10) that Christ died to provide for us. Too often we hear other people equate sin with socially unacceptable behavior. But Scripture has much to say that clarifies the nature of interpersonal sins (hate, unforgiveness, greed, envy) as well as intrapersonal sins (fear, unbelief, and so forth).

Our search for freedom will begin by seeing how freedom eludes us in the first place. We're going to get to the source of the problem. As the search for freedom continues, I'll challenge you to identify any strongholds that may have established themselves in your life. You may know of one or more now, but you're likely to discover some additional ones along the way. Only then will you be ready to begin to confront them. Don't get impatient. You first need to see clearly what your strongholds are and how they have gained such tremendous control before you start doing battle. In fact, if you try to fight them without understanding them, you're liable to do more harm than good.

I don't know where you stand, emotionally and spiritually, as you read this book. But I do know that you cannot move on if you don't first know where you are. If you call people on the phone and ask for directions to get to where they are, their first question will be, "Where are you now?" That's my question for you as you begin (or continue) your search for freedom. Don't assume you know. Be sure. I challenge you to adopt the plea of David when he prayed, "Search me, O God, and know my heart; test me and know my anxious thoughts. See if there is any offensive way in me, and lead me in the way everlasting" (Ps 139:23-24).

Eventually, I will propose a plan for destroying all the obstacles that stand between you and freedom—the only plan I've found that is effective in removing strongholds completely. I promise you there is hope for whatever you're facing. I can't promise the process is going to be easy or painless, but I assure you that any discomfort that arises in honestly dealing with your strongholds will be far less than the potential recurring pain they will inflict if you don't demolish them.

We're conducting a *search* for freedom. This search will require more than your eyes. You'll also need to prepare your heart and mind for what's ahead. In addition to knowledge, you'll need the courage to act on what you discover to be true.

In this book, we will see how the depravity of our flesh causes strongholds to occur. The next chapter will demonstrate how these strongholds form as a result of behavioral patterns begun during childhood. You may have noticed that many older adults still exhibit behaviors and emotions similar to those of children. We must break free from these patterns and strongholds in order to find the freedom our hearts desire. So take a deep breath. Pray for wisdom. Set your heart and mind for action. When you're ready, let's go.

Exercises for Chapter 1

1. Go through the following list and ask God to search your heart and reveal how your thought life could be described in each of these ways. It is important that you write out your responses; if not here, then in a personal diary or journal.

   EXAMPLE:
   ANGRY   *Every time I think of my sister and how she is more popular and pretty than I am, I feel angry.*

   SELFISH

   LUSTFUL

   DECEITFUL

   STUBBORN

   REBELLIOUS

   UNGODLY

2. During the next few days, be attentive to accounts of people who exhibit vile and degenerate behavior. As you read and hear these stories, remind yourself in each case that your flesh is no less evil and no less corrupt.

3. This is a process. As the days go by, be aware of any additional thoughts to add to step 1.

CHAPTER 2

Stuck with Childhood Patterns

S cripture clearly teaches that all people are born captives to sin. But as we have seen, many of us are unaware that we have been born into a fallen race in a fallen world that is an evil system unto itself. And to complicate matters, we rely upon our "flesh"—a corrupt and depraved part of us—to come up with ways to deal with the pain we experience in this world. Common sense should tell us that the coping mechanisms we develop as small children, will not continue to be effective as adults. Physical and spiritual maturity *should* be accompanied by a change in the way we handle problems and behave under stress. Too often, however, this is not the case.

Tom, for example, is a bright tax attorney who has been a friend of mine for many years. As far back as he can remember, he was ridiculed by his parents and friends. To deal with the pain of this, he withdrew. He built "internal walls" to protect himself from being hurt by anybody again. One day while visiting Tom's home, I listened to some of his wife's frustrations and then asked her a simple question: "After years of marriage, do you really know Tom?"

She thought for a moment, sighed, and said, "No, he never lets me get that close." I explained that it wasn't her fault. I had known Tom for years. I considered us friends. Yet he was a very "closed" person who had never revealed much of what was in his heart. After his wife stopped taking Tom's emotional distance so personally, she was able to accept him more than she ever had before. In return, Tom gradually began to let her into his life, and they continue to work on a more intimate relationship.

Physical and spiritual maturity *should* be accompanied
by a change in the way we handle problems
and behave under stress.

Tom is an example of someone with a problem that limits millions of men and women—his life, relationships, and self-image all continue to be strongly influenced by patterns he developed during childhood.

WORLDS APART

When we are very young, we develop patterns of responding to two worlds: our inner world and the outer world. For most of us, the inner world of our thoughts, dreams, feelings, fears, and imagination is even more powerful than the outer world of people, places, and things. As we move through each world, we encounter pain and pleasure. Although we gravitate toward that which gives pleasure, pain is usually a much greater motivator. This is especially true of emotional pain. Most of us accept the fact that we will encounter *physical* pain from time to time, but we are much more resistant to any kind of *emotional* pain. Sometimes the pain overwhelms us, and normally we gain little if anything by experiencing this kind of pain. The way we respond to emotional pain creates the most important behavioral patterns we have. It is, in fact, these patterns that create the core relationship problems in our lives.

In Tom's case, we see a person who could have enjoyed relating to others (pleasure), but the greater force in his life was to avoid the same kind of pain he had experienced in his relationship with his parents. The closer he got to someone, the more fear he would experience. When he reached a certain level of intimacy, he would simply shut down to avoid the fear.

These patterns develop at a time when we are in poor condition to make good choices. To help you grasp this, let me use as an example something that happened a few months ago when I had my appendix removed. While in the hospital, my attention was riveted to one of two things: either the pain I felt or the relief that the morphine brought. Many of my friends called or visited during the hours following my surgery, or at least they *told* me they did. I don't remember some of them.

Let's suppose a person called several days after my surgery to inform me that he had visited shortly after my operation and that I had signed all types of business agreements. Some of these arrangements, as it turns out, were extremely detrimental to me. As you might expect, I would not accept the legality of any documents I signed or verbal agreements I made. I would have such decisions set aside on the basis that my reasoning was extremely impaired. Both my visitor and I would clearly know this to be true.

Yet there was a time in my life when my judgment was even more impaired than during my recent post-surgery haze. It was during the first several years of my life. My thought processes were essentially dictated by those around me. Other people taught me what they believed to be truth (or, at least, what they wanted me to *think* truth was). Eventually, these truths became absolute convictions—about myself, the people around me, and the world in general. These basic convictions then became *patterns* of responding to myself and to other people. I can tell what I really believe by how I *respond* to life, not what I say I believe.

Here is how the process usually works:

Stage 1:   We are born and know little if anything about truth.

Stage 2:   As we're growing up, the people around us teach us
            what life is all about:
            Who I am
            Who to trust
            What's good or bad
            What I am worth
            What life and this world is all about... and so forth.

Stage 3:   The things we are told become a system of beliefs upon
            which we evaluate all new incoming information accept-
            ed or rejected as we compare it with our basic beliefs.
            Basic Beliefs vs. New Information

Stage 4:   Our definition of "truth" becomes whatever it is that
            we have been taught, and our beliefs begin to dictate
            our behavior. Then, as other people respond to our
            behavior, their responses tend to reinforce what we
            believe to be true.

As Tom went through this process, here's what happened.

Stage 1:   Tom knew nothing about truth at birth.

Stage 2:   One of his beliefs as a boy was that he was not good
            enough to be loved and accepted and that eventually
            the people close to him would reject him.

Stage 3:   He establishes and attends to relationships in life that
            validate his feelings of worthlessness and his expecta-
            tions of rejection.

Stage 4:   He tries to protect himself by not getting close to others (denying them the opportunity to reject him). In essence, he rejects them first. Then, when they "reject him back," their rejection confirms what he has come to believe about himself.

THE PROBLEMS WITH PATTERNS

Again, understand that beliefs based on childhood patterns are not reasoned out logically. If you doubt this, listen to the conversation of two children who have been taught opposite information about a topic. For example, listen to them argue over the rules of a game. Each will be totally convinced that he or she is correct.

Beliefs based on childhood patterns
are not reasoned out logically.

In addition to being devoid of logic, our basic beliefs and subsequent response patterns are not developed out of a relationship with God. Scripture has a vivid description of people who choose to ignore God: "Their thinking became futile and their foolish hearts were darkened" (Rom 1:21). And even when we don't intentionally choose to leave God out of the process, the result is the same. The definition of "truth" established during early childhood and the resulting behaviors usually precede a person's spiritual awareness. Our young minds are hungry for new information and quickly soak up whatever our parents or other authority figures tell or model for us. We respond to the world as adequately as we know how—but these are *responses of the flesh.*

Incidentally, this is how "the sin of the fathers" can cause their children to suffer to the third and fourth generation (see Exodus 20:5). Clinically, we see these patterns being passed from one generation to the next, often coming from the homes of alcoholics. Two of the classic patterns of the alcoholic personality are to control others and take responsibility for nothing. Sometimes children who are never addicted to alcohol will still exhibit these two characteristics and pass them on to their children.

Even though problems always arise when people use fleshly responses to the troubling situations of life, most Christians have never truly challenged their thinking. If a thought occurs, especially if it occurs several times, then they accept the thought as valid. This was the case for Beverly.

Beverly just couldn't seem to tolerate any conflict. She grew up trying to never say anything that would contradict anyone. In fact, she felt that her parents wanted her to do whatever anyone asked of her unless it was illegal. That had become her definition of being a nice, polite girl.

By the time she was forty-one, Beverly was severely depressed and unable to cope with day-to-day interaction with her husband and four children. Her husband, Tim, had almost given up trying to have a normal family relationship because Beverly refused to work through any conflict to reach a solution. When problems arose, she would give in to whatever the kids wanted, then sink again into her depressed state.

Sometimes Tim would get so frustrated that he would yell at Beverly. His anger only triggered a feeling that God might shout at her too. But eventually Beverly remembered an early childhood event that had been repeated until it became a behavior.

When Beverly was a child and felt unhappy, her mother wouldn't tolerate a sad demeanor. She always told Beverly to "put on a happy face" until Beverly came to believe that *feeling* bad was the same as *being* bad. So Beverly learned to smile and act happy in order to please her mother—no matter how she really felt.

But Beverly soon discovered that "a happy face" would not eliminate all her problems. One day she wanted to give her mother a present and innocently picked a bouquet of flowers from the neighbor's garden. She had no sooner gotten home than the neighbor's call of complaint about the little intruder sent her mother into a tirade. The spanking that ensued left flowers strewn across the floor as well as a numb awareness that, "No matter what I do, I can't please Mommy."

This moment was one that changed Beverly's life and influenced her self-image and behavior for years to come. She began to believe that she was supposed to please everyone but that it was impossible to do so. She wasn't permitted to be angry, and if she tried to form an opinion of her own, someone might get angry with her. Intellectually, she knew that God didn't have the same unreal expectations and harsh responses as her mother, but emotionally she felt that he did.

Years later, as a forty-one-year-old wife and mother, Beverly had another moment that changed her life. This time she decided to confront her false beliefs, one by one. She began to ask God what he *really* thought about her and to read God's Word with the determination to discover the actual truth. She started to see how great her fear of failure was and to what extent her craving for other people's approval allowed them to control her. Whenever she discovered a false belief, she rejected it and replaced it with God's truth.

Gradually and tentatively, Beverly began to express her real opinions in conversations with her family and friends. She found that even when her opinions led to conflict with others, her honesty also led to richness in her relationships. Beverly is still working on being herself and dealing more openly with others, and her only regret is that it took her so long to break out of the behavior patterns she formed while trying to please her mother.

OUT OF HIDING

Some things that children learn and quickly assimilate are easy to detect. It's evident that they haven't actually thought through the issue but rather are repeating what they've been told (repeatedly) is the truth. For example, young children of racist parents will frequently adopt the parents' prejudices automatically. There's no questioning as to whether Mom and Dad might be wrong. In fact, in order to feel secure, children must see their parents as being good and right. It's simply assumed that whatever they say must be true. Patterns quickly develop where "we" are always right and good, and "they" are always wrong and bad.

These patterns are simple to observe. But other, more subtle, issues may remain hidden. Children may loudly repeat certain statements they've heard Mom and Dad say, secure that they will receive affirmation. But if the message they've been receiving is, "You are a worthless excuse for a human being," they will be much less eager to admit it. Children hold those feelings inside, looking for ways to keep them hidden and to cope with them. As in my friend Tom's case, such hidden pains stemming from feelings of worthlessness can continue well into adulthood. And if action is not taken to change that childhood message, its negative influence will have destructive power throughout the person's life. The more people have learned to live with the problem, the more unlikely it becomes that they will attempt to overcome it.

> Even though children outgrow or otherwise
> get away from the original source of the problem,
> their behavior continues to be strongly influenced
> by the ongoing childhood response patterns.

Are these methods of avoidance and withdrawal wrong for children like Tom who were repeatedly criticized by insensitive or even abusive parents? Not at all. It's a natural defense mechanism that spares the child from pain.

But what begins as an instinctive and effective means of coping becomes a *pattern*. The child grows up, moves away from the verbally abusive parents, and begins to receive affirmation from others. *But the response pattern remains.* It is the established means of responding to others, and it will not easily be changed or removed. Even though children outgrow or otherwise get away from the original source of the problem, their behavior continues to be strongly influenced by the ongoing childhood response patterns.

It is as though children become emotionally stooped and hunched over. Adopting that internal posture keeps others from seeing them as any kind of threat, and therefore they are left alone. But now they are adults who stand straight on the outside but inwardly are still stooped and hunched over. Sadly, I see many people whose outer posture is excellent, but inside they remain distorted due to incredible fear of other people and life itself.

Tom found a devoted wife who truly loves him. Not everyone is so fortunate. Yet Tom continues to struggle. Even though his situation is far better than that of many people with similar problems, his patterns of withdrawal keep him from experiencing the full depths of joy and freedom in a loving relationship. He cannot open up to other people—not even his wife.

I will discuss other harmful patterns besides withdrawal later in the book. You may be experiencing one or more of them. For now, however, simply try to see how some of these problems originate. In most cases, it certainly wasn't your fault, yet it's now your problem. And it's a problem that won't go away until you determine to do something about it.

You can be free of the childhood patterns that continue to affect you in powerful and mysterious ways. But before moving ahead, spend some quiet moments thinking back to your own childhood. First, ask God to allow you to recall how you tended to handle problems, criticism, stress, and similar situations. Try to detect how you may be using any of those same coping methods today, as an adult. Then ask God to reveal how these childhood patterns are causing many of the problems you currently struggle with.

THE POWER OF DISTORTION

Finally, to understand ourselves we must recognize how our cognitive processes have become distorted. Distortion occurs at several levels as we assimilate information. It begins with our perceptions.

We have a limited capacity to take in new information. Suppose you go to a party and walk through the roomful of people. You will be able to acknowledge only a small fraction of the action that is taking place around you. Some people are better at this than others, but no one comes close to observing everything that is going on. It is as if you have a mental grid that takes in certain things and excludes others. Typically, this grid reflects your expectations, which are determined by past experiences.

Let's say you are going to a company party. You've been to several of these before where you felt that the top executive seemed to ignore that you even exist. You may not intentionally feel that you will be ignored at this one, yet something in your mind—your "grid"—expects this. We expect history to repeat itself. It is entirely possible that unless the top executive drops everything he is doing to personally give you his full attention, you will leave the party feeling ignored again. In truth, perhaps you will subconsciously ignore all his attempts to get your attention.

We see only part of the picture called life. It is like a giant puzzle where we see a few pieces and try to fill in the rest on our own. How would we do if we were given one thousand jigsaw puzzle pieces with no idea of what the completed puzzle was to look like? We would probably be doing a lot of guessing. Occasionally we might guess right, but I think more often we would be totally wrong. This is like the dilemma we face as we try to cope with life based on our limited perceptions. To various degrees, the "grids" in our minds distort the things we see.

To make matters worse, these distorted perceptions are then fed into a distorted processor. I was among the first wave of people with a fascination for computers. I got my first one in the mid-seventies, and convinced a friend to allow me to put the books of his small gift shop onto my new computer. But something was wrong with my early model. It put one person's charges on another person's account. By the time I noticed what it was doing, I had invoices spread all over my house in an attempt to try to straighten things out. The store owner has never forgiven me for the mess I made of his books. I wanted to do a good job. I tried very hard to do everything just right. But my intentions and efforts were not enough. Because there was something wrong with the software that ran the computer, I made a great mess of the whole project.

Scripture declares that we are born with a fouled-up processor. It doesn't matter how much we want to be excluded from this fact of life or how hard we try to work with what we are born with. No matter what we do, our understanding is limited.

Since our perceptions are distorted and the way we process information is distorted, is it not logical to assume that many of the patterns of behaving and expressing feelings are going to be distorted as well? We do the best we can, but we must conclude that many of our current patterns of behavior may well be erroneous.

If you are beginning to understand what I'm saying, I believe you're in the minority. Even people who have been Christians for years struggle with these issues every time I speak on the topic. They do not understand what they need to be free from, much less how to become free.

FAMILY FEUDS

Perhaps nowhere are faulty patterns of behavior as noticeable as in families—usually in other people's families. We tend to see the shortcomings of others much more quickly than we do our own.

For example, I spent one Christmas with a family who had a lot of other relatives drop in to visit. The visitors must have thought that the longer they stayed, the bigger their presents would be. After a few hours, the family I was staying with began to get desperate. They didn't know how to get rid of their uninvited guests.

Their solution was to go to a local cafeteria for dinner. That way they would all eat together, but then each family could go their own way. This dinner was certainly an eye opening experience for me. I discovered that my hosts had unwritten rules for every nuance of life. Apparently, this was especially true of what you did or didn't get at a public cafeteria.

We all have certain behaviors in life that we just never think to question.

Their rule was that in order to show proper restraint, a person should get only three items with each trip through the line. It didn't matter what three things were taken, but they were firm about the three-item limit. Can you guess what happened? The visiting family members loaded their trays until they couldn't carry any more.

Nothing was said during the dinner, of course, and everyone said their good-byes amicably. But for days afterward, the visiting family members were the topic of conversation. It seemed to have been a small matter that they had worn out their welcome. But taking more than three items in the cafeteria—now that was offensive. By doing something that broke this family's "rules," the visitors had dropped to the approximate level of slime in the eyes of their hosts.

As I soon found out, this family had rules about almost everything. You either lived your life their way or you were considered essentially worthless. There seemed to be little variance in the degree of importance of the rules. All that mattered was whether or not a rule—any rule—was broken.

We all have certain behaviors in life that we just never think to question. We may not be counting cafeteria dishes, but I predict that we're doing something equally unusual.

In the next two chapters, we will take a look at both childish behaviors and emotions. I expect that by the end of these two chapters we will begin to discover that in many ways we may still be children. I realize this will be hard for some of us to consider. But if we want to put away childish things, we must face what those things are.

Exercises for Chapter 2

1. How did your family feel about each of the following issues:

    *   The importance of family

    *   Hard work

    *   Lazy people

    *   What to do on Sunday

    *   What not to do on Sunday

    *   Purchasing used items or wearing hand-me-downs

    *   Doing activities together as a family

    *   Eating meals together

    *   How holidays should be celebrated

    *   Hair length for boys and men

    *   How money should be earned, spent, and saved

    *   Music

    *   Curfews for teenage children

    *   Allowances

- How to choose friends

- What age to date, wear makeup, drive the family car

- Importance of getting an education

- Importance of marrying someone with an education

- Interracial dating and marriage

- Interreligious dating and marriage

- Humor

- Importance of good manners

- Poor people

- Elderly people

- Abortion

- Politics

2. Go back through the previous list and put a check mark beside all the areas where you believe the same way your parents believe(d).

3. How did your family perceive you? (Mark all the words that seem correct.)

Furious	Daring	Intelligent	Inferior
Irritated	Fascinating	Confident	Inadequate
Skeptical	Stimulating	Thankful	Miserable
Bewildered	Amused	Sentimental	Stupid
Aggressive	Extravagant	Serene	Bashful
Discouraged	Delightful	Responsive	Jealous
Insignificant	Cheerful	Relaxed	Selfish

Weak	Satisfied	Pensive	Apologetic
Foolish	Valuable	Agonized	Arrogant
Embarrassed	Worthwhile	Apathetic	Frustrated
Hateful	Appreciative	Hostile	Critical
Hopeful	Angry	Rejecting	Important
Indifferent	Blissful	Faithful	Rageful
Confused	Nurturing	Mad	Helpless
Trusting	Scared	Submissive	Exhausted
Insecure	Loving	Joyful	Anxious
Fearful	Powerful	Cautious	Intimate
Obstinate	Excited	Thoughtful	Optimistic
Sexy	Grumpy	Peaceful	Energetic
Content	Sad	Determined	Sleepy
Prudish	Disapproving	Bored	Withdrawn
Playful	Lonely	Puzzled	Creative
Guilty	Relieved	Aware	Depressed
Vulnerable	Proud	Ashamed	Undecided
Respectful	Shocked	Disgusted	Happy
Suspicious	Envious	Hurt	

(Adapted from Gloria Willcox, "The Feeling Wheel.")

4. Go back to all the adjectives you marked and circle the ones that are also true of the way you now feel about yourself.

5. How do you react to stress and conflict? (Use the adjectives on the previous list to respond. Then, as an optional confirmation, have someone who knows you well go through your list to see if he or she agrees.)

6. Which of the words you used to answer question 5 are also true of the way you responded to stress and conflict as a child?

7. How do you determine if what you think is actually true? How often do you catch yourself thinking something and then rejecting those thoughts because you recognize that what you're thinking is false?

CHAPTER 3

Childhood Behaviors

L et's envision an imaginary scenario. You're selling a house and decide to consult a lawyer to handle all the paperwork. At random, you pull a name out of the phone book (because the office is near your home) and make an appointment to see Ms. Young of the Young and Childs partnership.

You arrive, and the reception area is formal and classy looking. The receptionist is courteous and efficient. But when you are shown into Ms. Young's office, your first impression is you've mistakenly found the nursery. The wallpaper contains bold patterns of dolls, puppies, and baby bunnies—all in pastel colors. A large rocking horse sits in the corner. A number of teddy bears are lined up on a shelf above the credenza of legal files. The bookshelf contains, in addition to the law books you would expect to find, a large assortment of coloring books, oversized picture books, and a number of children's classics (*Curious George, Mother Goose, Good Night Moon,* and many others).

You begin to assume that perhaps this law firm specializes in children's cases, and you wonder if you can get a good referral to a business lawyer. Then Ms. Young comes in. She is about forty years old and dressed in a professional-looking gray business suit. You're quite impressed with the way she carries herself... until she utters her first words: "Sorry. I had to go potty."

Now you're confused. Your eyes quickly search the wall. Yes, there it is, a law degree—from Harvard Law School, no less. Ms. Young certainly seems to be qualified to help you. But still, things seem to be getting "curiouser and curiouser."

Ms. Young motions for you to sit down and asks, "Would you like some tea?" After you nod, she pulls out a pink plastic tea set and pours imaginary tea into your pink plastic teacup. "Lemon and sugar?" she asks. *Why not?* She spoons invisible sugar into your cup with a pink spoon and squeezes an imaginary lemon. She blows into her cup and says, "Be careful. It's very hot." Finally she takes a sip of "tea," sits back in her expensive leather chair, takes a long satisfying breath, and asks, "Now what can I do for you?"

From all appearances, Ms. Young has the training, experience, references, clientele, and all the other qualifications you'd expect from an attorney. So how do you think you would feel about doing business with her? I would venture to guess that most people would be more than a little uncomfortable trusting her with delicate legal matters. Her flashes of childish behavior would likely put off most of us to the point of questioning her capability, regardless of all her other credentials.

But don't you know people similar to Ms. Young? Oh, they aren't usually as blatant as Ms. Young about displaying their childish behavior, yet you see enough indications of it to know for a fact it's there. See what you can observe in the lives of the following three people.

John's been married for fifteen years, but he still flirts with pretty women and leers at younger ones. When it comes to relating to the opposite sex, he still behaves the same way he did as a hormonally controlled high school student. His wife used to be embarrassed by his behavior, now she's just sad. Other people, however, are uncomfortable when they're around John when he models his adolescent attitude toward women.

Sara could always depend on her parents to give her everything she wanted. Well, her parents aren't around anymore. And before long, the money she inherited from them won't be either. But Sara still spends her time traveling, shopping, and looking for other people like herself to hang around with. Without a husband or job, people are wondering how much longer her "free ride" will last. She doesn't give it much thought.

Troy was "one of the boys" who went out drinking every weekend in college. The other "boys" eventually became men. They graduated and went to work. But Troy kept looking for the weekend party action. And he kept drinking—by himself when no one else was around. He now tries to find work, but the priority he puts on his partying weekends is having a stronger and stronger effect on his working week.

John, Sara, and Troy are searching for freedom, but they are doing so in childish ways. At one time the "lusts of the flesh" such as sexual activity, self-centeredness, and excessive drinking seemed to give them some relief from lives that seemed otherwise shallow. Now those fleshly answers don't seem to work anymore, but they keep trying them because that's all they know to try. Their search for freedom takes them deeper and deeper into various kinds of bondage.

You probably know people like John, Sara, and Troy with similar, and equally disturbing, problems. It's quite unsettling to see someone beginning to reveal gray hair and wrinkles who still reveals ridiculously childish behavior as well.

BEHAVIORS WE NEED TO OUTGROW

Although most of us do better than John, Sara, and Troy at hiding it, we know of certain childish behaviors that we have not yet outgrown. They are usually the behaviors that seem to be so negative in our relationships. Below are a few examples.

Temper tantrums. Ever watch parents being trained by their children? Smart kids know the temper tantrum is one of the most effective tools they can use. To be effective, temper tantrums must be thrown with great abandonment. The flinging of arms and legs while screaming at the top of the lungs is usually effective for both embarrassing the parent and obtaining the desired goal. To throw a tantrum correctly, the child must appear to really "lose it." The tantrum must be so violent that the parent doesn't even consider trying to reason with the child.

Although these shows of force are designed to obtain something immediate and specific, they have a much greater goal as well—control. When the tantrums are erratic, control can be obtained most effectively. If the parents aren't always sure what triggers the tantrum, they're never quite sure how to deal with them.

Joe was a handsome older man. His graying hair gave him a distinguished look. But Joe died a lonely old man who was both feared and loathed by his children. As an adult, he had perfected the tantrum that he learned during childhood. He applied it with great skill to his children and his wife. They never knew just what would set him off, so they were always on pins and needles. After his death, his children were left with memories of a volatile and violent man, but there was also a deep sadness. Joe had been a man of great wealth who had experienced much success. However, in doing so he had alienated all those around him. In the end, he was a man to be pitied because he had never grown up.

Crying. It doesn't take long for some kids to break out in bursts of uncontrollable crying. They learn that grown-ups don't usually know what to do with a kid who is exhibiting such deep hurt. In fact, crying usually pays off with lots of attention since the people around become very accommodating. If being a regular kid doesn't do the trick, show everyone you're a *fragile* kid.

Molly had been fragile all her life. Now she couldn't seem to help herself anymore. If anything unpleasant occurred in her life, she just fell apart. As she got older, it seemed to take longer for her to recover. So if her husband was foolish enough to try to discuss one of her behaviors he felt was offensive, by the time she would "come out of it," he could barely remember what he had wanted to talk about. Of course, the day came when he really needed to discuss issues that were essential to the health of their marriage. But he couldn't communicate through her tears. So eventually he found someone who would listen to him and not demand to be treated like a china doll. Molly still cries a lot. But now there's nobody around to hear her.

Whining. I don't know why God gives kids such high voices. I'm sure he wearies of hearing them whine. Unlike a tantrum thrower, who sounds something like a tornado siren, the whiner is more like a dripping faucet. The whining can be ignored for a while, but eventually something has to be done about it. Whining, when combined with an "Oh, pitiful me" approach, can get a lot done for children that the children ought to be doing for themselves.

Mildred was an excellent whiner as a kid. Now as an adult she's even better. You can tell she's a pro, because she hasn't found anything she hasn't been able to complain about. Most people might stop whining when they reach the top 10 percent of the social-economic strata and have an attentive spouse who is one of the hardest working people you'll ever meet. Yet to hear Mildred, you'd think she was one of the five most ill-treated women in the world. She can't recall the last good day she's had.

Most people can tolerate her for short periods of time. It's those close to her who suffer most. That's probably why her husband works so hard. It's easier to work longer hours than to figure out how to satisfy Mildred. Her children hate to hear the phone ring. So many times in the past they've answered, only to hear her latest tirade. She seems to be waiting for someone to make her miserable life better. She'll probably die waiting. No one cares any more. Besides, no matter how they might try to help, it won't be enough.

Clinging. At times, all children need special attention from the people closest to them. It seems appropriate for children to cling to parents when they get sick, when something goes wrong during their day, or in other crises. However, some children never get past the intense need to be comforted. This symptom sometimes indicates that the child has experienced some kind of trauma. But other times clinging is actually encouraged by a parent who does not want the child to feel any independence. Clinging can be detected in various ways in adult life, but probably one of the most common is in romantic relationships.

Lana never seemed to be able to get enough attention to satisfy her. She had been a precocious child and a flirtatious teenager. Desperate for more and more attention, her flirtations quickly became a pattern of sexual promiscuity. As soon as she could, she found a husband whom she thought could finally give her the "love" she thought she deserved. (Frankly, she wanted someone to adore her twenty-four hours a day.)

Luckily, she found a husband who liked to feel needed. They seemed to be a perfect match—for a while. But problems arose later on when he began to mature and Lana didn't. There were times when he needed to receive attention, but Lana didn't seem capable of doing to others what she wanted done for herself. The marriage eventually broke up. Lana's still looking for another person to cling to.

In some cases, when a relationship like Lana's is threatened, or when the stronger of the two decides it's time to "get a life," the tension leads to "mental breakdowns" or even suicide attempts on the part of the clinging person. Such things seem to be the last remaining options for attracting attention.

Bickering. In some families, particularly those with numerous children, bickering becomes a common behavior. Some children try never to allow a sibling to gain any advantage. Bickering is a tool used to wear down "the opposition."

Bobby is a case in point. He was so good at bickering as a child that he became a renowned lawyer who was quick on his feet and even quicker with his mouth. Now he presents his case and never gives an inch. He's not a whiner; he's an in-your-face kind of guy. No one can ever remember him saying "I'm sorry" or "I made a mistake."

Bobby could be a charmer if he needed to be, and he had attracted a lovely wife. Yet when it came to social relationships, they were never on anyone's short list of friends. Though Bobby could be fun, he was usually much more of a pain to be around. He seemed to enjoy intimidating and harassing even the most secure people in a group. His positive points were never enough to outweigh his bickering. No one really *likes* Bobby. Unless he changes, he will only be tolerated.

Strong-willed defiance. It's good to see children stand for their principles, but some children never sit for anything. It's as though they're afraid that someone will take away their oxygen if they ever give in. Even if parents also have strong wills, strong-willed children usually triumph because the children have more energy. And children don't usually select particularly good cases to take a stand on. But it's as though they have some kind of internal switch that, once it goes on, stays on until they get what they want. That was Betty's problem.

"I'm not going to change," Betty said defiantly. She was on her third marriage, due largely to several self-centered behaviors that seemed minor to others, but Betty treated them like life-or-death issues. She insisted on having her own way whenever and wherever she wanted. The wishes of her children and ex-husbands didn't seem to matter.

Betty was a nice-looking and intelligent woman. It was simply amazing to see her make the same mistakes over and over again in her life. But woe to the person who ever offered support. It seemed impossible for anyone to break through and help her. She resented such efforts because she felt threatened by them.

Being the continual center of attention. Leslie was one of those children who caused everyone to marvel at her talent. In addition, she had a natural sense of humor and a lot of poise around adults. Her relatives always said she could become a star if she tried because she was such a delight. Of course, her sisters didn't feel she was so delightful. They were justifiably jealous because of all the attention she received. With Leslie so good at everything, what would be their niche in the family? Besides, she treated them like her personal servants.

Today Leslie is in her late thirties and is still the center of attention. She still looks young and is more beautiful than ever. She married a wealthy older man and is a prime example of a "trophy wife." She looks as good on his arm as his fancy cars look in his driveway. (Of course, while she is his "showpiece," he has other women to appease his sexual appetite.) They go to elite charity balls—she in her elegant gowns, he in his tuxedo. People stare at them and wonder what it's like to be so special. But Leslie has reached the point where she wonders what it would be like to live a normal life. It's hard for her to imagine. As the center of attention, she's right where she always wanted to be—or so she thought.

Irresponsibility. Few children are by nature responsible individuals who automatically pick up after themselves, do their chores without being prodded, and so forth. Responsibility must be instilled as a value for most of us. But sometimes parents find the lackadaisical traits of certain children so endearing that the children are never forced to take responsibility for themselves.

These childish behaviors are
not only unattractive, they are
potentially destructive.

Robin was one of those individuals. His mother went through the motions of telling him to clean his room, set the table, and take out the trash, but he always had a good excuse, so she would do his chores for him. When he got older, however, he discovered that his first boss (at a fast food restaurant) was not so accommodating. He soon quit to find a "good" job. He quickly went through several jobs and bosses. His teachers weren't any more merciful. Though everyone acknowledged his boyish charm and his propensity for play, they couldn't overlook his inability to do what was required of him. He never made it through school and he has just about stopped looking for work. He still lives at home where Mom continues to take care of her "little boy." But now she's starting to worry because at her age it requires more and more effort just to take care of herself.

These childish behaviors are not only unattractive, they are potentially destructive. The apostle Paul declared that there is a manner of speaking, thinking, and understanding associated with our childhoods that should be *left* in childhood: "When I was a child, I talked like a child, I thought like a child, I reasoned like a child. When I became a man, I put childish ways behind me" (1 Cor 13:11).

Adults widely expand their vocabularies, learn to drive, get married, go to work, have families, and perform any number of "adult" actions, yet they can remain childish. I believe Paul's reference to "childish ways" applies to three major areas: (1) the way we have been taught to communicate with those around us; (2) the way we have learned to process information coming to us; and (3) the way we organize our world. Let's look at each of these areas in greater detail.

COMMUNICATING WITH THOSE AROUND US

Each of us has learned his or her own individual way of communicating, both verbally and nonverbally. Most of our communication—by far—is nonverbal.

Children, in particular, tend to communicate nonverbally, especially with adults. They don't have the confidence, maturity, and verbal skills to sit down and have an in-depth discussion with parents or other adults. So they find other methods of communication: nonverbal ways to persuade, complain, express feelings, and so forth. I know I did.

As a child, I learned to communicate by using my emotions. My specialty was sadness. I could "do sad" until the flowers wilted—well, at least until my mother gave in. For example, I remember wanting to see the first episode of *Have Gun, Will Travel,* a program of obvious cultural importance to a child growing up in the "wild west" of Oklahoma. The only problem was that my parents didn't seem to share my intense desire to see this show, and the only television available to us was three miles away at my grandparents' house. It didn't take long for me to conclude that my verbal plea was falling on deaf ears.

However, I was far from through. I took my beat-up rubber ball and trudged off to play a little solitary basketball. I had nailed a coffee can with the ends cut out to the side of the tool shed. Fortunately for me, it was strategically placed where my mother would be sure to see me. I emitted sad feelings that would have rated at least an eight or nine on a ten-point Pity Meter. Sure enough, my mother couldn't stand it. She gave in, and that night I happily watched my program.

My method of communication was effective during childhood, so I tended to communicate the same way as an adult. Instead of verbalizing what I wanted people to understand, especially if they had made me angry or sad, I would simply emote it. This is an extremely dysfunctional way of relating to others. Emotions may continue to get results, but they don't *communicate* thoughts or needs. As a child, my tactic wasn't necessarily a bad one. It was probably the only way I could convince my parents (who tended to be insensitive to my needs) to respond to me. But as an adult, I needed to put that childish way behind me.

I have counseled many "emotional communicators"—people with childhoods similar to my own who have allowed destructive patterns to develop in their adult lives. Some look as if they have been using the same emotion so long that their faces have frozen in that position. They need to break free of those childhood patterns that have come to control them.

As you look back over your life, perhaps you will see similar patterns. What once was an instinctive and perhaps ingenious pain-avoiding technique may now be your worst problem—a destructive pattern that prevents you from enjoying the fullness and freedom of life. (We will deal with additional specific patterns in later chapters, but it's enough at this point to see how such problems begin.)

PROCESSING INFORMATION

Not only do many adults communicate in childish ways, they also tend to think in childish ways. Most children think in contrasting terms. They see people, things, and situations as being either awful or great. If something isn't terrific, it's terrible. If it's not personally agreeable, it's distasteful. As children mature they learn that many things fall somewhere along the continuum between the two extremes. In life they will face a lot of "gray areas," average relationships, so-so circumstances, and other "in-between" experiences.

However, many people never outgrow their black-or-white thinking. As a result, friends can quickly become enemies. Heroes fall and become goats. Positive experiences suddenly become unacceptable situations. And friends or family members who witness such sudden changes in opinion are wary about forming close relationships with people whose attitudes can shift so quickly. I have met thousands of people who cannot allow themselves to enjoy life because they are so disturbed by what is not "right"—things that seem insignificant and inconsequential to everyone else. Samantha was such a person.

Many people never outgrow
their black-or-white thinking.

Samantha had a beautiful new home, much more spacious and expensive than her previous ones. But the first week she spent in her new dream house was a miserable one. A carpenter had made a mistake when he put a handle on the hamper in an upstairs closet— a spot that no one would ever see except her daughter (who couldn't have cared less). But Samantha was so angry that she couldn't enjoy everything else that was wonderful about the house.

This may seem like an extreme and ridiculous example, but if we are to "put childish ways behind us," we must consider more than our actions. What we *do* is important, yet what we *think* is even more so. We cannot consistently behave as adults until we quit swinging from one extreme to the other and instead learn to process information logically and rationally.

ORGANIZING OUR WORLD

We learn primarily by category and association. If I tell you I have a pen in my pocket, you wouldn't know if it is a Bic or a Mont Blanc. But you still have an idea of what I'm referring to. Why is that? Because you have a category in your thinking titled "pen." It is a general category, yet specific enough for you to list several characteristics: a writing instrument, long, pointed tip, uses ink of some sort, etc. How did this category *originate* in your mind? At one point when you were quite young, you were introduced to an object that you were told was a pen. Soon the category was formed, and as you came into contact with other pens, this category became solidified in your thinking.

Now suppose what might happen if something had been wrong with the first pen you ever had. Let's say its plastic sheath had been cracked, and it pinched your finger every time you tried to write with it. And let's suppose that this happened often enough so that you began to associate "pens" with "pain." In your childlike way of thinking, you could assume that all pens are the same. You would tend to avoid them, believing that they all caused pain.

Let's look at another analogy of childish thinking. Put yourself in the place of a young girl whose father does not fit the definition of what a "father" *should* be. Perhaps the man is neglectful or verbally or physically abusive. His repeated actions, witnessed by the young girl, would quickly become a source of pain. And because the father is a man, perhaps the girl begins to categorize all men as sources of pain and grief. She will not usually be aware that she has done this.

Later in life the young girl might meet someone who seems very different from her dad. She gets married, but one day this man who had seemed so special does something to hurt her feelings. She feels pain, and something inside her concludes that she had been wrong about thinking that this person she married was different—all men *are* alike. It's much easier for her to revert to her original (childish) definition of men, even though it was quite distorted, than to endure the occasional discomfort and conflict required to establish a more realistic definition.

This problem is true for young boys trying to define "women" as well. Consequently, many young husbands and wives, after getting married, cannot understand the "hatred" they encounter from a spouse. Occasional conflict is certain to be part of every marriage, but people working with wrong (childish) definitions are going to have much more difficulty working through those conflict situations. They may be paying for the sins of their own parents or even the parents of the spouse.

A major requirement of "putting childish ways behind us" is going through our "mental dictionaries" and reevaluating the way we define basic concepts of life: *love, anger, masculinity, femininity, forgiveness, help,* and much more. Some of the definitions may be perfectly OK. Others, however, are likely to need significant revision. Many people live and die while naively holding to faulty definitions established during the early years of childhood. Such people never experience the level of freedom that could be theirs.

One way to recognize our faulty categories is to notice our responses—especially our negative ones. Often we will react to a situation with much more energy than we would have expected. This usually means the situation is somehow connected to something in our past that remains unresolved. Harry, for example, forgot his wedding anniversary one year. His wife Charlotte was not just mad; her anger continued to consume her for days thereafter. As Harry kept seeking her forgiveness, Charlotte finally told him that as a child her birthdays were sometimes ignored, but her brother's birthdays were *always* celebrated. Because Charlotte had never been healed of her childhood pain, she reacted as if Harry was treating her as her parents had.

One of Henry David Thoreau's most often quoted statements is, "The mass of men lead lives of quiet desperation." I believe he is right. We don't always know exactly why we feel the way we do or what needs changing. We just feel the despair. And since we're uncomfortable with the feeling, we keep it to ourselves. How sad!

In your search for freedom, don't settle for "quiet desperation." Analyze the things we've been dealing with in this chapter. Can you detect "childish things" associated with your patterns of communication? Do you need to adjust the way you process information, in being less extreme and expanding your gray areas? Do you need to reorganize your world and redefine your outlook toward the people you come into contact with?

There can be many joys and benefits associated with childhood. But when it comes down to it, children can never be truly free. Children must always depend on other people for survival. Only those who are capable of making decisions and acting on them can experience freedom. Yet with such privileges of adulthood come the necessities of determining truth, facing reality, and making necessary changes in one's thoughts, actions, and attitudes. It's not usually easy. But the longer changes are put off, the harder it becomes to change. I encourage you to *commit* now to making any needed changes—even though the actual *process* of change is likely to take a while.

Exercises for Chapter 3

1. Below is a list of some of the behaviors that can make children unpleasant to be around. Select the five behaviors you tend to find most annoying.

Temper tantrums	Disrespecting others
Crying	Blaming
Whining	Clinging
Asking inappropriate questions	Fidgeting
Squirming	Asking too many questions
Bickering	Hyperactivity
Difficulty remaining seated	Easily distracted
Talking too much	Not completing activities
Not doing chores	Not listening

Being strong-willed	Losing books and toys
Carelessness	Popping gum and blowing bubbles
Tattling	Being too daring
Talking too loudly	Interrupting
Arguing	Exaggerating

2. For each of the five activities you checked above, write out how the childish behavior can translate into adult behavior. For example, a child's temper tantrum might consist of lying on the floor, kicking and screaming. An adult might instead yell and use every known curse word.

3. How do you respond to adults who use behavior like that you just described in question 2?

4. In what ways do you act childish?

5. How do you think others respond to you when you revert to childish behavior?

6. Do you automatically respond to certain situations with childish behavior? What does this tell you about your behavior patterns?

7. What are some of the ways you communicate that might be ineffective?

   EXAMPLES: Glaring glances
   Saying *"If you really knew me, you would know why I'm mad."*

8. Do you have a tendency to think in extremes—to relate to life as either all good or all bad, either wonderful or horrible? If you have trouble answering this question, ask the advice of someone who knows you well.

9. Review your answers to question 1 at the end of chapter 2. Spend some more time thinking about the things you were taught as a child, and how those things may still affect you today.

CHAPTER 4

Emotions of Childhood

S uppose I, with my great intellectual genius, create a pill that will prevent you from ever having a fever again. One dose is all you need to be fever-free for the rest of your life. How much would you be willing to pay for my marvelous discovery?

Wise people would never take such a pill—much less pay for it. A fever isn't pleasant, but it plays an important role in our lives. A fever signals that something is wrong. When we realize we have a fever, we have advance notice that our bodies are not operating correctly. We can then begin to monitor our progress, take the appropriate medication, and see a doctor if necessary. We become clearly aware of our situation, and we have a number of options to pursue that will help take care of the problem. Eliminating a fever, the warning signal, would make us extremely vulnerable to things that are much worse than the fever itself.

Now let's consider an alternative. Suppose I offered you a one-time pill that would eliminate every negative emotion you might ever experience from now on. Would you consider taking *this* pill?

It's amazing how many people answer yes to this second possibility. We usually see the purpose of pain on a *physical* level. Yet when it comes to our *emotional* state, we seem much more eager to avoid any and all unpleasant feelings. But the principle is the same: negative emotions can be God's signal to us that something is amiss and needs attention. If we can learn to properly understand our emotions, we will begin to thank God for the negative feelings and then seek to get to the source of them.

IDENTIFYING OUR FEELINGS

A counselor might use the following tool to help people get in touch with their emotions. Why would people need help identifying their emotions? Because most of us have never been taught how to deal with our emotions, especially the negative ones. We learn to handle physical pain, even if our solution is simply to endure it. But emotional pain causes a number of other problems we don't seem willing to tolerate.

Take a look at the chart on the facing page, and then we'll consider some of the problems that arise when trying to deal with emotions.

People who feel emotional pain many times do not know how to identify it, much less what to do about it. Some people seem to think that it is wrong to feel negative emotions, and expressing such feelings is definitely out of the question. A tool like this chart can help people become much more specific about how they feel from day to day, and even from moment to moment.

I have seen people exhibit every signal that they were angry (short of steam coming out their ears), yet they vehemently denied it. Perhaps they felt anger was one of those feelings that "nice people" don't experience. Or perhaps they thought that if they

How Do You Feel?

	Lonely			**Belonging**	
left out	isolated	separate	popular	important	influential
friendless	withdrawn	rejected	famous	well-known	valuable
forsaken	lonesome	withdrawn	needed	accepted	worthwhile
lost	insignificant			attached	

	Angry			**Peaceful**	
furious	mad	frustrated	calm	collected	composed
hacked off	hard	boiling	quiet	sedate	cool
aggravated	irritated	indignant	serene	content	tranquil
distant					

	Sad			**Happy**	
dejected	depressed	gloomy	joyful	glad	bright
unhappy	cheerless	glum	ecstatic	pleased	vivacious
dreary	blue	downcast	cheerful	delighted	elated
woeful	grieving	heavy	upbeat	light	bouncy
sleepy					

	Afraid			**Secure**	
anxious	fearful	scared	safe	optimistic	hopeful
frightened	shocked	terrified	protected	sure	confident
alarmed	unnerved	timid	stable	poised	assured
jumpy	tight	shaky			

	Hateful			**Loving**	
hostile	critical	jealous	tender	accepting	loyal
unfriendly	quarrelsome	spiteful	affectionate	kind	sympathetic
mean	nasty	hostile	warm	devoted	caring
harsh			forgiving		

	Inadequate			**Powerful**	
weak	bashful	inept	strong	great	sure
small	meager	powerless	energetic	dominant	aggressive
useless	deficient	vulnerable	assertive	pushy	confident
			upbeat	assured	intoxicated

	Guilty			**Innocent**	
ashamed	damned	judged	pardoned	set free	naive
criticized	doomed	trapped	pure	released	acquitted
cursed	dirty	embarrassed	forgiven	exonerated	justified
			clean	fresh	

(Adapted from chart titled "How Do You Feel," author unknown.)

admitted their angry feelings, they might then be expected to do something about them.

I've also seen several men who repeatedly denied being sexually attracted to women. They eventually had to deal with the truth, and in many cases the truth was acknowledged only after marriages had been destroyed. Had they been willing to be honest early on, they could have prevented the problem from getting worse. But they waited until the emotions were so overwhelming that they became all but unstoppable.

Logic and intellect are just as fleshly as emotions.
I've seen people who are just as much slaves to
their cognitive thinking process as other
people are to their strong emotions.

Other times emotions are distorted by a "charade factor." People might be angry to the point of rage, yet refuse to call the emotion "anger." Instead, they might only confess to feeling "frustration." Those people cannot deal with their anger until they properly identify the emotion. Other feelings that hide behind charades are *indifference* posing as "boredom," *lust* posing as "love," *disgust* under the guise of "distaste," and *withdrawal* being dealt with as "shyness."

HOW DO WE HANDLE OUR EMOTIONS?

When dealing with emotions, people tend to go to one of two extremes. At one end of the scale are the people who believe that emotions are potential problems to be overcome. Proponents of this position operate from a cognitive and logical position, encouraging people to ignore their emotions. Since emotions are part of our "flesh," they say, we should simply not allow them to have any sway in our lives. What these people don't understand is that logic and intellect are just as fleshly as emotions. I've seen people who are just as much slaves to their cognitive thinking process as other people are to their strong emotions.

At the other extreme is the belief that we should just "go with" whatever we feel at the moment. Let emotions run rampant. Teachers of this position recommend such things as expressing anger by beating pillows while cursing at the top of your lungs. They feel that the goal is to rid your system of a negative emotion like you would vomit a poison out of your stomach. Their solution has been proven faulty, however, because expressing anger in this manner becomes both enjoyable and rewarding at a certain level. Consequently, the approach doesn't work at all in diminishing anger and other strong emotions. Rather, people actually begin to act out their anger more often.

It's much more reasonable to acknowledge that our emotions are obviously given to us by God. Scripture teaches that we are not to be dominated by our emotions. Our emotions expose us to the things that are taking place in our souls. If we ignore them, we lose valuable information that could direct us. If we let our emotions run wild, we will live our lives erratically.

Negative emotions, like fevers, serve as warning signals that something is wrong. To do away with them would be a tragic mistake. We need to learn what our negative emotions are trying to tell us.

WHAT'S STOPPING YOU?

Some of you may be wondering, "So what's the big deal? If you feel a lot of anger, you find out what's causing it, deal with the real issue, and watch the anger dissipate. Right?" Essentially, that's the goal. Yet it's rarely that simple.

After reading the previous chapter, you may agree that many people (including yourself) are responding to life according to childhood patterns rather than how they might *choose* to respond. So why don't they just stop doing what they don't want to do and start doing what they *do* want to do?

Is it ignorance? Perhaps so, for a while. They might remain unaware of the pattern in their lives for a long time. Yet discovering the problem is certainly not an automatic solution. Some people see a destructive pattern repeating itself over and over again yet can't break out of the "usual" response. Clearly, the problem isn't ignorance.

Is it indifference? Do people simply not care that they are controlled by childhood patterns? I don't think so. I've met hundreds of people who are miserable because they are unable to break out of childish patterns. They care desperately that they can't seem to straighten out their lives.

If I'm trying to remove an old brick barbecue from my patio I can use a sledgehammer or a Nerf bat. In both cases, I will exert a lot of energy in trying to tear down the obstacle. The difference is that by using the sledgehammer I will eventually accomplish my goal.

Is it laziness? Do people feel it'll take too much effort to do anything about the problem? On the contrary, most people exert immense amounts of energy in trying to deal with their problems. Sadly, their efforts are usually misdirected. Some try to keep the problem hidden. Some try to keep it from getting any worse. Some do their very best to confront and eliminate the problem. But sometimes the methods they use simply will not accomplish what they are trying to achieve. If I'm trying to remove an old brick bar-becue from my patio in order to build a new one, I can use a sledgehammer or a Nerf bat. In both cases, I will exert a lot of energy in trying to tear down the obstacle. The difference is that by using the sledgehammer I will eventually accomplish my goal. Using the Nerf bat, I never will. Now if my goal had been to hit a Nerf ball, the Nerf bat would have been the correct and preferable tool. So it's not that people are using worthless tools and tech-niques to combat their emotional problems, sometimes they're sim-ply using the wrong ones. And they are working very hard as they do.

So if it isn't ignorance, indifference, or laziness that prevents people from changing their childish behaviors and moving on with their lives, what is the problem? I believe it's *fear*.

The hold our childhood patterns have over us can be compared to drug addiction. As small children we occasionally face unpleas-ant, and even traumatic, situations. We have no idea how to respond, but we do the best we can. We withdraw. We become rebellious. Or in an effort to make everyone happy, we become as perfect as possible. And our tactics seem to work—at first. But with time, the behavior becomes less and less effective. Like the person who uses drugs, the person caught in a fleshly childhood pattern is imprisoned by a stronghold. Even though they no longer desire to behave a certain way, the person seems powerless to change the behavior. He or she has grown so dependent on the source of the problem that it is a difficult and frightening proposition to imagine living without it.

I think fear, in one form or another, usually is why people contin-ue to live with childhood patterns rather than to "put childish ways behind them." Several years ago I wrote a book titled *The Search for Significance,* in which I described several fears that begin during childhood and continue to influence us as adults. The next few pages summarize some of that information because I believe it will help you in your search for freedom. If this is new to you or a bit hard to understand, I strongly encourage you to read *The Search for Significance* and deal with these issues in more detail.

THE TYRANNY OF FALSE BELIEF

Our fears often arise from false beliefs we have about ourselves or the world around us. I'd like to examine four false beliefs and the fears that result from each one.

1. I must meet certain standards in order to feel good about myself. Satan loves this definition of success, and then we denigrate ourselves and demolish our self-esteem because we are never as successful as we think we ought to be. We stop being satisfied with doing the best we can. The fear of failure consumes us.

The New Testament Pharisees had established an elaborate system of legalistic rules and regulations and had convinced themselves they were living up to the high standards they had set. When Jesus came along, however, he frequently pointed out how they were deceiving themselves and others as well. But rather than consider that he might be right, the Pharisees refused to admit their shortcomings. They eventually had Jesus killed rather than concede that what he said was true. Many people today try to live up to their own standards of perfection.

Ben, for example, grew up in a good Christian home. His mother was supportive of her three sons, but his father was a quiet man who said little. He wasn't abusive, but he didn't offer the praise and affirmation they needed either. Ben was confused about the mixed messages he received. He felt so good when he did something that brought a shower of praise from Mom that he became driven to elicit a similar response from Dad. Before long, Ben was excelling in school, in athletics, at church, and in all aspects of being a good son. He worked much harder than his two younger brothers and did everything he could to impress his father, but his dad never noticed or acknowledged Ben's efforts.

Ben continued to do well in college. After graduation he married a nice woman and started a family of his own. He also entered the ministry, quickly moving from a small rural congregation to a large and prestigious suburban church. He was young to command so much responsibility, but everyone was impressed with how hard he worked and how well he did.

But the truth is, the ministry was probably the wrong place for a person like Ben. He was still a hands-on person who saw a job through until it was done right. But when is the ministry of a large church ever "done"? Ben wasn't good at delegating responsibility. He would work long hours preparing sermons, meeting with numerous committees, and seeing to the smooth operation of the church. At night he would conduct personal visitations to hospitals, recently bereaved families, and people who had attended the church for the first time.

Everyone was impressed with Ben's dedication. But to Ben it seemed that there was always something else to be done: Members needed his counseling, new building projects needed his time and energy for planning and fund-raising, and homeless people were begging for help. The demands for his time went on and on. How could he ignore any of these good people and projects?

As a child, Ben had determined to impress his father. When his father died, he was proud enough of Ben but had never made a big deal over him. Of course, the father had never expressed much approval for any of his sons. Ben, however, was the only one who took it so personally. He felt that he had failed to earn his father's approval, and he was going to make sure he never failed again.

Ironically, the harder Ben worked to be the ideal pastor, the less time he spent with his own children. By the time he got home at night, even if his kids had stayed up to see him, Ben had little energy left for them. The oldest son is starting to try harder and harder to capture Ben's attention and hear a few words of praise from him.

Do you see the cycle?

God's unconditional love and forgiveness is made available to us, not because we ever get good enough to earn it, but because Christ died on the cross to make it possible.

Most people get caught up in a performance trap of one form or another. Some become much more perfectionistic than others, but the problem is widespread. The result of this false belief that certain unwritten (and unreasonable) standards must be met leads to the fear of failure. As they grow older some people stop trying anything new for fear of failing. They don't realize that those who never fail can never succeed either. Success in life is a matter of trial and error. Without occasional—perhaps frequent—errors, a person never grows. And a person who never grows can hardly be considered a success.

Fear of failure can also lead to anger and resentment, anxiety, pride (based on one's self-worth), depression, low motivation, sexual dysfunction, and chemical dependency. The fear of failure causes emotional pain, and people will try any number of things to eliminate, or at least reduce, the pain. The trouble is that they don't deal with the source of the problem, so the pain always returns.

God offers the only lasting "antidote" to the fear of failure. We, with all our fleshly wisdom and strength, cannot deal permanently with the problem. We must turn to God for his answer: *justification.*

God sees the pain and problems caused by an ongoing fear of

failure. And he patiently waits for us to come around and see what truly needs to be done. But if we feel that nothing we do will ever be good enough to satisfy ourselves, how can we be expected to be good enough for God?

The moment must come when we realize and truly believe that our salvation has nothing to do with how well we perform. God's unconditional love and forgiveness is made available to us, not because we ever get good enough to earn it, but because Christ died on the cross to make it possible. The moment we put our faith in Jesus, God attributes Christ's worth to us. He no longer sees us as condemned sinners. He literally adopts us as children who are fully pleasing to him. This is the essence of justification.

From that point on, nothing we do—no amount of success and no amount of failure—can affect God's love for us. Of course, we need to deal with our sinful actions, words, and attitudes, but not because doing so will cause God to love us more. We seek change so that we can become more like Christ. Therefore, we must learn to step forward in faith and confidence that God will see us through our failures. We have nothing to fear from him. And with God's love and power in our lives, we eventually come to see that we need not fear failing in front of people either.

People who are afraid to fail are perhaps the ones who will most appreciate the truth of Romans 5:1-2: "Since we have been justified through faith, we have peace with God through our Lord Jesus Christ, through whom we have gained access by faith into this grace in which we now stand." Usually people must first will themselves to believe this at a cognitive level. But with time, prayer, and faith, this truth becomes heartfelt, and the fear of failure gradually dissipates.

2. I must be approved (accepted) by certain other people to feel good about myself. This belief leads to a fear of rejection.

You probably know people who conform their attitudes and actions to the expectations of others. You may do so yourself. You may do it without realizing it. Many times this is why people join social clubs and organizations.

But, fear of rejection makes it almost impossible for people to have meaningful relationships. Friendships remain superficial because it's too painful to risk intimacy when rejection might be the ultimate result. Eventually, for many people, this fear leads to a life of isolation. As the fear becomes greater, the more distant people become from those around them. A hermit never faces rejection from others. Of course, a hermit never faces others. But avoiding rejection, a person also avoids good conversation, shared laughter, working together for common goals, and so much more that life has to offer. This was true for Joann.

Joann is a pastor's wife who was also a pastor's daughter. When I met her, I thought, *This is one pastor's wife who has it together.* But that was part of the reason she had come to see me.

Joann told me she felt lousy about her role and had little affection toward her husband. As she talked, she was surprised at the bitterness she felt toward the ministry. She recalled her father who led every church service with a loving and caring attitude, but all too frequently, took out his frustrations on his family in the privacy of home. Her mother was the target of significant verbal abuse, and young Joann was sensitive to her pain. She referred to her childhood existence as a "double agent life." She always felt that she must behave perfectly and not show anger toward anything.

Joann is thirty-nine years old, and all but five of those years have been lived in a parsonage. She told me, "It's like being owned by the congregation." For example, she had overheard church members chastising her mother because weeds grew in the flower bed by their front porch and, after all, "the parsonage belongs to the church."

Joann's own children have serious problems. When her son took up with a rebellious group of friends and her daughter ran away, Joann was amazed. She thought, *I never had the nerve to do even harmless things I wanted to do because I wanted so much to avoid any criticism. Now look at my children!*

Her family was visibly falling apart. She admitted feeling sick and tired of being unable to be herself. She said that as the pastor's wife, "I have no identity of my own." And her husband didn't understand what she felt. Joann was hurt and angry when he scheduled a camp speaking engagement and called it their "family vacation." Another time when the kids would be out of school for spring break, he scheduled an out-of-town revival meeting. She felt he was making major decisions without her and not communicating them until it was too late to do anything.

When Joann and her husband came for counseling, I asked, "Why don't you leave the ministry or find a different kind of ministry?" Joann was furious at first. After all the years she had devoted to the ministry, how could anyone suggest they leave now? But with time, Joann thanked God she was given that option to think about. A light bulb came on in her mind. On one hand, she was afraid that her life had been lived for nothing. But she also became aware that she still wanted to be a pastor's wife.

Eventually she admitted that she was still angry about the insensitive people who had criticized her mother years ago. She was also angry with some of the people in their current church congregation. She said, "I feel like I've been held hostage for years." She also confessed to feeling rebellion and passive-aggressive thoughts. "I would sit on the back row of the church instead of the front row as expected. I thought, *I'll show them. They expect me to sit up front.*"

Joann began to see that her problem was bitterness, not the ministry itself. Before she could experience the freedom she longed for, she had to acknowledge the connection between her current situation and the painful memories she had of her childhood. She had to forgive the old offenses. She also decided to confess her anger and bitterness—and the sorrow it had caused her—to her church family.

She and her husband composed a letter together. She read the letter during a Sunday morning service and then told the people, "This is what my life is like. Don't feel sorry for me. I'm sorry for my offenses against you. Please forgive me."

Joann knows there will always be people who criticize weeds in her flower garden, but she's working on not letting her fear of rejection make her entire life miserable. She knows she can respond correctly to the things she thinks and feels. Now when she feels bitterness or anger, she immediately goes to her heavenly Father and tells him she recognizes that it is sinful and that she doesn't want it to grow. She forgives the offender and thanks God for his way of dealing with anger and bitterness. She depends on his Word rather than the word of others for guidance and consolation. She's starting to see why the Bible warns us not to let the sun go down on our anger (see Ephesians 4:26-27). She says, "Now when I go to bed without resolving my angry feelings, I spend half the night thinking about it. If I don't do something about the anger, it robs me of rest and peace."

Her honest evaluation of herself helped her acknowledge that her lifelong fear of rejection caused her to feel like a failure—first as a preacher's kid, and later as a preacher's wife. But she now chooses to bring her fears and hurts to light and try to see them from God's viewpoint. She tells God right away when she is upset with others—or even with him. And she is growing and becoming more free with each passing day.

Joann's symptoms are typical of someone struggling with a fear of rejection: anger, resentment, hostility, being manipulated by others, codependency, avoiding people, an urge for control over others, and depression.

God's answer to the fear of failure is an awareness of his justification; his answer to the fear of rejection is *reconciliation*. When Christ died for our sins, he provided much more than our justification. We also find forgiveness, reconciliation with God, and total acceptance. Reconciliation means that those who were at one time enemies have become friends. We see the significance of our reconciliation with God in Colossians 1:21-22:

Once you were alienated from God and were
enemies in your minds because of your evil behavior.
But now he has reconciled you by Christ's physical
body through death to present you holy in his
sight, without blemish and free from accusation.

If the fear of rejection has plagued you, dwell on this promise of reconciliation for a long time. Find someone who can discuss it with you. Try to truly believe that because of reconciliation, we are completely acceptable *to* God and completely accepted *by* God. We can forget about trying to perform for others. God's opinion is what matters most, and we can always be sure that he will never reject us.

3. Those who fail are unworthy of love and deserve to be punished. Those who hold this belief fear punishment.

Fear of punishment permeates a lot of people's lives. Many of us work at a place where assigning blame for what goes wrong seems to be a favorite pastime. We frequently catch ourselves doing the same thing—trying to point a finger at someone else before other fingers begin to point at us. And there may be plenty of times when we can find no one else to blame for what is going wrong, so we end up pointing a finger at ourselves. If no one else is around to punish us, we kick into a self-blame mode. Or we assume people are angry at us.

Liz, for example, is a quiet young woman of thirty-four who comes from a strict family. Her father was a heavy-handed disciplinarian who was critical of everyone—especially Liz, her three sisters, and her mother. As hard as they tried, none of them could do enough to please him. Any time one of the family members did something wrong, they could expect to hear about it. The father wasn't excessively violent, but he made it clear when he was unhappy: raising his voice, rolling his eyes, slamming doors, giving lectures, and so forth. Liz and her family had many times been punished for insignificant offenses.

As an adult, Liz had worked for ten years as a secretary at a large firm. She was competent and well liked, but during that time she had developed an ongoing emotional struggle. Almost every day at noon, her boss would ask her to pick up a sandwich for him while she was out. Her lunch periods were typically hectic times when she rushed around catching up on her own errands and hurrying to make it back to her desk in her allotted time. She didn't mind doing a favor for her boss, yet she felt angry that he had taken it for granted that she would use *her* short lunch break to take care of getting *his* meal.

One day it struck her how angry she was, so she decided to deal with the situation. To her surprise she saw that she was relating to her boss like she had responded as a little girl to her demanding father. She saw that she feared punishment, even though there was no longer any apparent reason for this reaction.

Liz thanked God for revealing this truth to her. She realized she needed to resolve her resentment toward her father before she could do anything about her work situation. She asked God to show her all the ways her bitterness was controlling her. She told God she didn't want to be bitter any more. She soon began to see her childhood situation more objectively and chose not to interpret her father's severe judgment of her and others as justified personal attacks. Liz determined she would no longer allow her childhood relationship with her father to control her.

After working through many of these issues, she prepared to deal with her work situation. The next time her boss requested a sandwich at lunch, she took a deep breath and cautiously told him she just didn't have time. To her surprise, he understood. His reaction was nothing like what she had expected—nothing like her father's loud vocal outbursts. Liz took a big step toward freedom when she was able to risk suffering disapproval from an authority figure in her life.

Liz demonstrated most of the effects of the false belief that failure deserves punishment. Interestingly, self-induced punishment is one of the major symptoms of this fear. Subliminally, we feel that if we punish ourselves enough, then God won't need to punish us. Other symptoms are bitterness, passivity, and a tendency to punish others.

How did Liz overcome the fear of punishment that had controlled her life since she was a little girl? She found God's answer: *propitiation* (which simply means that the wrath of someone who has been unjustly wronged has been satisfied). This book started out discussing how we as human beings are sinful and depraved. In our fleshly nature, we commit sins that are offensive to God. But because Christ died on the cross as our substitute, we are not punished. Christ took upon himself the righteous wrath of God that we deserved.

Below are two passages that clearly describe Jesus' act of propitiation.

This is how God showed his love among us: He sent his one and only Son into the world that we might live through him. This is love: not that we loved God, but that he loved us and sent his Son as an atoning sacrifice [propitiation] for our sins. Dear friends, since God so loved us, we also ought to love one another.

1 John 4:9-11

Surely he took up our infirmities and carried our sorrows, yet we considered him stricken by God, smitten by him, and afflicted. But he was pierced for our transgressions, he was crushed for our iniquities; the punishment that brought us peace was upon him, and by his wounds we are healed. We all, like sheep, have gone astray, each of us has turned to his own way; and the Lord has laid on him the iniquity of us all.   **Isaiah 53:4-6**

Christ took upon himself the punishment we deserved. Does it not make sense that he would also want to help us overcome fear of punishment that we *don't* deserve?

4. I am what I am. I cannot change. I am hopeless. This deception gains strength every time we base our self-worth on past failures, dissatisfaction with personal appearance, or bad habits. It gets stronger with every failure. Some people try diligently to overcome their problems but find themselves unable to do so. Eventually they give up and resign themselves to a life devoid of joy or freedom. How can they ever feel free if they believe that change for the better is impossible?

Intense emotions result from this false belief. One of the most prominent is shame. We know what kind of people we really are. We know what kind of people we should be. And we know that nothing we do seems to propel us from one point to the other, and consequently, we feel shame.

In order to be free of shame, we need to change our self-concept. We need to learn to relate to ourselves in a new way. To accomplish this, we must begin to base our self-worth on God's opinion of us and trust in his Spirit to accomplish change in our lives. Then and only then can we overcome this destructive lie.

Lisa came to me for help after overdosing on sleeping pills. She was filled with despair, guilt, and depression. Her wrinkled and soiled clothing were additional evidence of her inability to take care of even routine activities. She hesitated many times as she told me her story, barely mustering enough energy to give all the details.

Beginning at age six, Lisa was sexually abused on a regular basis by her stepfather. This deviant relationship was the only understanding she had of things such as intimacy and the love of a father.

Though Lisa was just a child herself, she began to imitate her stepfather's behavior by abusing her younger brothers and sisters. She taught them the sexual behavior that had been imposed on her. All of her siblings eventually had inappropriate sexual encounters during their teen years.

No one knew about the abuse that Lisa struggled with. She couldn't bring herself to trust any male figure, and feared intimacy.

When Lisa was ten, she began to sense that what was happening to her was wrong, and she totally withdrew. At about the same time, her mother and stepfather divorced. Her mother remarried, and her new husband genuinely loved Lisa (who was fourteen) and the other children. He had two children from a previous marriage, and he wanted to build a secure family life with his new wife and her children. But he found a big wall of resistance, especially from Lisa. She remained distant.

No one knew about the abuse that Lisa struggled with. She couldn't bring herself to trust any male figure, and feared intimacy and sexual situations with men. She even considered lesbianism— going to the extreme in her sexual identity—but she never acted on those thoughts.

Lisa's fear and distrust of men led to a fear of God as well. By the time I met her, she was staying away from anything that might lead to a relationship with *anyone.*

For most of her life Lisa felt depressed, guilty, and ashamed. She couldn't rid herself of those emotions, and they had finally driven her to overdose. Tearfully she told me she deserved punishment for abusing the other children in her family.

Lisa began to attend a support group for survivors of sexual abuse. She tentatively started to participate as a member of the group as her trust in other people was gradually rebuilt. God used this group to show her that she didn't have to carry the shame she felt. She learned to make new choices. She confessed her sin and asked God to help her overcome her hesitancy in trusting others and especially in considering *herself* trustworthy. God understood everything she had suffered. He bound up her broken heart.

Not everyone's past experiences are as graphic or as painful as Lisa's, but they don't need to be. We can feel shame for a small offense. Anything that makes us feel worthless and helpless can open the door for these destructive emotions to come in and take over our thinking. They cripple us emotionally. Shame is usually the ringleader of these emotions, but so can inferiority, habitually destructive behavior, self-pity, passivity, isolation and withdrawal, loss of creativity, codependent relationships, and an extreme dissatisfaction with (even to the point of despising) one's personal appearance.

What is God's solution for gaining freedom from shame? In a word, *regeneration*. Regeneration is not a self-improvement program. It is not a cleanup campaign for our sinful natures. It is not a positive-thinking alternative. Regeneration is nothing less than God's impartation of a new life for us. The amount of change we can expect is no less drastic than the difference between life and death: "Because of his great love for us, God, who is rich in mercy, made us alive with Christ even when we were dead in transgressions" (Eph 2:4-5).

Can God's regeneration make a difference in *your* life? Read the following passage and decide for yourself.

At one time we too were foolish, disobedient, deceived, and enslaved by all kinds of passions and pleasures. We lived in malice and envy, being hated and hating one another. But when the kindness and love of God our Savior appeared, he saved us, not because of righteous things we had done, but because of his mercy. He saved us through the washing of rebirth and renewal by the Holy Spirit [regeneration], whom he poured out on us generously through Jesus Christ our Savior, so that, having been justified by his grace, we might become heirs having the hope of eternal life. **Titus 3:3-7**

BEYOND THE FEARS

I hope you are beginning to see how important it is to stay in tune with your emotions. It does no good to deny what we're feeling, to give nice names to negative emotions, or to suppose that if we ignore them, they will go away. God can and will provide whatever we need to get beyond our painful emotions, but *only if we are willing to be honest about them.*

That's why the four fears I have just presented are so devastating. They evoke a response from us that may reflect the way we responded to our childhood fears. When you were a small child and were afraid of something, what was your first instinct? Most of us closed our eyes. If we feared monsters in the closet, we hid under the sheets of the bed. If we feared something we saw on TV or at a movie, we covered our eyes with our hands. And for many of us, this childish response to danger and unpleasantness has followed us into adulthood.

When one or more of the four fears entrench themselves in our lives and keep us from experiencing freedom, we may close our eyes to the potential pain and danger. When we do, we don't see the problem clearly. And if we don't see the problem clearly, we can't get rid of it.

God can and will provide whatever we need
to get beyond our painful emotions, but only
if we are willing to be honest about them.

I urge you to peek between your fingers long enough to understand what you're afraid of. What is it that's keeping you from moving forward toward freedom? It may be one or more of the fears and false beliefs that you've just read about. Many times the various fears are intertwined. When this happens, freedom becomes just that much harder to find.

It will take time, patience, and God's help to get past these fears. They started during childhood and have been gaining strength ever since, so don't expect them to suddenly disappear. Yet the sooner you begin to wrestle with the truth of what they are doing to you, the sooner you will be able to move ahead.

Our fears prevent us from taking action against our childhood patterns, and as you will see in the next chapter, our childhood patterns can grow into strongholds. As you read on, just remember that God *does* have solutions to get us past all our fears. All strongholds *can* be demolished. But before we begin to discuss the solutions, we need to take a look at how strongholds gain control over us.

Exercises for Chapter 4

1. Below is a list of fears. Check the ones you can identify with.

Failure	God punishing me	Abandonment
Rejection	God rejecting me	Being worthless
Other people	Failing God	Being useless
Animals	Dying	Making decisions
New experiences	Going crazy	Being a leader
Bad weather	Committing suicide	Criticism
Disease	Disappointing people	Being hurt
Storms	Losing control	Not being liked
Responsibility	Being incompetent	Nighttime
Hurting people	Darkness	Confronting people
God loving me	Being alone	Angry people
Weight loss	Not being loved	My own anger
The future	Anything new	Assertiveness
Talking before people	Trusting people	Taking risks
Talking on the phone	Being loved	Not measuring up
Men	Women	Being punished
Being transparent	Not being perfect	Women never changing
Standing up for myself	Ending up like my parents	Not being nice enough

2. List the fears you checked in the space below. After each one, explain how your life has been affected by that specific fear.

3. Review your list of personal fears, and designate with a *C* the ones that seem to have their origins in your childhood.

4. Place an *X* on the line below to indicate how frequently you feel guilt or shame.

   Never_____All the Time

5. Can you recall events from your life that occurred many years ago, yet still provoke guilt? If so, detail each of these on a separate sheet. Confess to God that you have not yet experienced the reality of your forgiveness, but that you desire to. (I would also suggest that you read *The Search for Significance* as well.)

6. During the next several days, make a list of things over which you "beat yourself up."

CHAPTER 5

Understanding the
Enemy Within

———▲———

By this point in the book, two things should be clear. First, in spite of how wonderful or horrible our family members might have been, we all were born into a race of evil and fallen people. Unfortunately, we have lost sight of what a serious term *fallen* is. Until we face this basic truth, though, we are tremendously handicapped as we understand ourselves and the world around us, as we interact with other people, and especially as we try to respond to the emotional pain we experience.

I also hope you realize that no matter how old we might be, *the choices we made during childhood probably continue to dominate our life experiences today.* As children we had no spiritual direction or development, so our childhood choices were made as part of a defective *process.* Yet as we made the same choices again and again, they became a defective *pattern* that can still wreak havoc in our lives today. We like to think we make new choices, but it would be closer to the truth to say we simply repeat the choices we've always made. Our patterns of choices are so consistent that they become extremely predictable. We think we've left childhood behind, yet we continue to carry with us the worst part of it—our childish responses to problems. Again, it is vital to accept this fact. If you have problems doing so, ask God for clear insight to see that this is the truth.

THE SOURCE OF STRONGHOLDS

As you dwell on these two truths, you should begin to understand the source and the nature of strongholds. A passage I will refer to throughout this book is 2 Corinthians 10:3-5:

Though we live in the world, we do not wage war as the world does. The weapons we fight with are not the weapons of the world. On the contrary, they have divine power to demolish strongholds. We demolish arguments and every pretension that sets itself up against the knowledge of God, and we take captive every thought to make it obedient to Christ.

My definition of a *stronghold* is "any area of our lives we cannot control that is destructive." According to the previous passage, *all our strongholds can be demolished.* So far I've written about the tremendous power of our destructive childish thought patterns. Yet these problems, as serious as they are, can be demolished. Healing can take place. Truth can replace faulty thinking.

You may think you've tried everything humanly possible. Perhaps you have, and that's the root of the problem. If the solutions you've tried have been "human" (fleshly), they have been ineffective. The destruction of strongholds requires more than your own strength and wisdom; it requires God's power. You will have to depend on the Holy Spirit first to reveal the strongholds in your life and then to provide the power to demolish them.

If we were to compare our thoughts with God's thoughts, we would quickly see there is no comparison:

"For my thoughts are not your thoughts. Neither are your ways my ways," declares the Lord. "As the heavens are higher than the earth, so are my ways higher than your ways, and my thoughts than your thoughts."
Isaiah 55:8-9

But we would recognize that our false reasonings and so-called knowledge isn't actually knowledge at all. We would see that our beliefs were formed as children, prior to salvation, when our minds were hostile to the things of God. It should come as no surprise, then, that the majority of our thinking is completely at odds with what God knows to be true.

Consequently, strongholds form. The very use of the word *strongholds* in Scripture should suggest that these are specific areas of life that are intense, require much energy, and dominate our experiences in life. Let's explore how strongholds are formed.

FIGHT OR FLIGHT?

Almost all emotional pain has something to do with key personal relationships. As a child, those relationships are usually with parents or other close family members. When children encounter pain in their relationships, they have essentially two options. They can *fight* to try to control the source of pain, or they can *flee* and try to get away from the pain. Children may have slightly different variations of the fight-or-flight options, but almost every response to pain will come down to one or the other alternative. And it really doesn't matter which option they choose. Either one will initiate events in their lives that will eventually lead to more pain. This additional pain leads to additional fighting or fleeing. This cycle continues until children form established response patterns. The patterns provide a degree of relief, but they always cause grief in the long run. Below are some stories that will illustrate some of the ways fight and flight responses can affect people.

When Ted encountered pain as a child, he used a classic flight response: withdrawal. Whenever conflict or tension erupted in his home, he would "disappear." Sometimes this meant closing the door to his room and only showing up for meals. Other times he would find reasons for being gone from home altogether. It's hard to say why he chose this pattern. Perhaps he saw a similar pattern in his father's life, or maybe he just tried it one day and found it was effective in lessening his fears and tensions. Choosing this pattern was by no means unethical or immoral. If you lived in his house, you would find no reason to blame him for his tendencies to withdraw. Yet, as we shall see, Ted would eventually experience much pain later in his life because he had learned to respond to conflict by withdrawing.

Ted met and married a young woman named Anne, who responded to conflict differently. Her whole family loved to argue more than eat. They were very emotional—screaming at each other one minute and embracing each other the next. No one knows how Ted and Anne went through their courtship without these extreme differences becoming apparent—and even derailing the relationship. Yet they did.

After they got married, Anne was confrontational when she

wanted to "talk things out." But the more she got in Ted's face to get his response, the more he would withdraw. Her confrontation triggered his pain, and his withdrawal caused her to feel resentment.

Ted soon learned to tolerate Anne's behavior by tuning her out and ignoring her. Anne learned how to push the right buttons when she wanted something from Ted. They are still together, yet neither really trusts the other. Although they have stayed married, they experience little of the "oneness" and satisfaction that God intends married couples to have. They are lonely, angry people.

We see the same symptoms of childhood patterns in the behavior of another married couple: Bill and Denise. A successful man, Bill seemed to be at ease in almost any situation. Few would ever guess that underneath the surface was a hollow man who was confused and had no sense of who he was.

Bill grew up with an overprotective, dominating mother. Bill was his mom's reason for living, and she made sure nothing ever happened to him. She would not even allow him to play with his cousins of the same age for fear that he would get hurt. When a parent is this domineering and protective, it leaves children without any identity. Children aren't capable of thinking through problems logically, so they subconsciously begin to think of themselves as inept—and grossly inferior—to require such a degree of protection. This wasn't the parent's intent, yet you can see how children might develop severe problems because of the parent's overprotectiveness.

Bill eventually escaped some of his mother's control, but he did so by learning to role-play. His natural abilities allowed him to become extremely successful at filling these roles, but Bill was still hollow inside. He tried to fill the void—sometimes with good, but at other times with hedonistic, self-gratifying activities. He could be a completely different person depending on his situation. Bill's role-playing, like Ted's withdrawal, was neither unethical nor immoral.

It was the only way he knew of escaping the domination of his mother. But, those childhood patterns almost ruined his adult life.

Bill later met Denise, who had been sexually abused as a child. She showed all the typical signs of the trauma she had gone through, the most pronounced being her tendency to dissociate. For an abused child, dissociation is the mind's way of escaping the horrendous things the body is enduring. However, it is a highly addictive response. Later in life the person will have a tendency to dissociate in self-destructive ways.

When Denise met Bill, she created an identity for him that wasn't at all who he really was. But Bill could usually play the role she had created. Whenever he didn't, Denise could just block out anything about him she didn't like. Their extremely dysfunctional way of relating worked for a long time. But when they started getting closer and Bill could no longer accommodate her expectations for him, they faced an inevitable conflict. She was angry because he wasn't the person she had tried to make him be, and he was confused because he had hardly changed his behavior before she began rejecting him. The methods they used to cope with pain as children eventually betrayed them. Those patterns simply would not work for adults.

"I CAN'T BELIEVE THEY'RE RELATED!"

Fight and flight responses can vary greatly within the same household. Some brothers and sisters who grew up in the same home can be extreme opposites. One can be the world's biggest chatterbox, while you can hardly get a word out of the other. One will be outgoing and athletic, while the other's nose is in a book the whole time. One is serious and somber most of the time, while the other could be a stand-up comic. In other cases, though, adult brothers and sisters act very much alike, right down to their choice of fight or flight.

For example, Gary was one of several sons whose father appeared to be a model parent. Among the community and his peers, Gary's father was perceived as hard-working, competitive, strong, and a loyal family man. Yet Gary's family members were among the few who knew how prone the father was to go into fits of violent rage. All the sons were victims of intense and repeated verbal and physical abuse. They could not fight since he was much larger and stronger, so they used the flight response. One "ran away" by lying about his age and joining the army early. Another found every conceivable hiding place on the property and would stay out of Dad's sight as much as possible. Others turned to substance abuse to distance themselves from the severity of the problem.

Today the brothers have various problems. Two became homosexual. One has other serious sexual problems. Another bought a mobile home and literally ran away to live alone in the woods. The father has been dead for years now, but the sons continue their patterns of flight, only with other people now. In one way or another, they continue to run from their father and everything he stood for. And while they have different specific problems, they are still very much alike.

Now suppose we have a home with a workaholic father who is usually absent. When he is around, he always takes good care of ten-year-old Jill and nine-year-old Erica, but those times are far too few and too short for little girls growing up. Sometimes Jill sees Dad for a few minutes at breakfast, but most days he is gone before she wakes up and doesn't get home until after she goes to bed. Even his weekends are full of scheduled business dinners and golf games.

Jill desperately wants her father to pay more attention to her; so does little sister, Erica. Jill chooses a fight response. She develops a performance-oriented mind-set and does everything within her power to "force" Dad to like her. She starts making straight A's in school. She goes out of her way to stay up later or get up earlier just to get a couple more minutes with him. She draws and colors beautiful pictures and cards to leave where Dad will find them. And while Dad appreciates her efforts and tells her so, there are no more hours in a day, so he doesn't spend any more time with her.

Erica, on the other hand, chooses flight. Rather than feeling that Dad has deserted her, she decides to leave him first. But a nine-year-old has a limited number of options for "leaving." She begins with a symbolic effort of packing up her stuff and "running away from home" but sees that's not going to work on a long-term basis. For one thing, she realizes she is dependent on Mom and Dad for necessities. For another, it is Mom (of course) who comes looking for her and chauffeurs her back home. She never accomplishes her goal of getting her Dad's attention.

So Erica "runs away" by retreating *inward*. When Dad does carve out a few minutes here or an afternoon there to spend with his daughters, she refuses to even get involved, much less excited. She starts spending more time in her room. When she is doing "family things" in the den or car, she has on Walkman earphones with the music at a sufficient level to tune out everyone else.

It wouldn't be surprising to find Jill in the same, or a related, field as her father. From all outward appearances, she may seem confident and personable. After failing to capture her father's attention as a child, she will see that most everyone else notices her. She's likely to be outgoing, determined, accommodating, and likable. And deep down inside, she'll still be hoping that Dad will notice her.

Erica, on the other hand, will probably continue her patterns of flight. She may want to make sure that the rejection she felt as a child will never touch her again. If so, she isn't likely to have any close friendships—especially not with men. The independence, or solitude, she carved out for herself will probably show up in her jobs, relationships, and overall personality. And throughout her life, she'll still be wishing that Dad would notice her. Erica and Jill are the kind of siblings you'll look at and think, "I can't believe they are sisters!"

Clearly, people can act in opposite ways for essentially the same reasons. And if Jill and Erica don't consciously do something to alter their responses to their father's neglect, their behavior will soon develop into a destructive pattern. But neither will simply grow out of the problem. It will be with them until they choose to deal with it.

Most people seem to prefer flight over fight. Remember, we are talking about *childhood* patterns. Rarely do small children think of opposing their parents. If something is wrong, it is common to distance oneself from it with withdrawal, despair, self-pity, lying, fantasies, role-playing, addictions, and so forth. As children mature, many continue the flight patterns already developed, and the problem intensifies as those behaviors are carried into adult life. Others turn and face the painful situation head-on—to fight back with stubbornness, rebellion, self-centeredness, violence, and similar behaviors.

OUR SUSPICIONS ARE CONFIRMED

Emotional pain readily reasserts itself in our lives. For example, children who are neglected or abused might think, at first, *It seems that Mom and Dad don't love me as they should. Maybe, just maybe, that's more* their *problem than it is mine. I know I'm doing everything I can to hold the relationship together.* It's a fairly healthy response, but it's not a strong one. The emotional pain makes it difficult to think rationally and logically. People feeling such pain are exceptionally fragile.

Then, one day, hurting children experience what I call a "crystallizing event." It convinces them that their suspicions about their self-worth have been right all along. And, if they were older and more aware, it would reveal to them that a damaging pattern has developed in their lives.

For instance, suppose Ken is the youngest of eleven children. His parents have to work double shifts to provide for all the kids. The older brothers and sisters do what they can to help around the house. It wouldn't be unusual, under such conditions, for Ken to struggle with feelings of abandonment. He might feel as if he were not important enough to warrant his parents' attention. But he understands, sort of, and gives Mom and Dad the benefit of the doubt because of his home situation.

Now let's put ourselves in Ken's place on the first day of kindergarten. A teacher and an assistant are striving to keep up with twenty-five scared and homesick children. They're doing the best they can to keep everyone's spirits up, but they can only do so much. If Ken isn't one of the few who receive some special attention that day, this might be his "crystallizing event." It might be the last straw that confirms in his mind, *I was right. No one thinks I'm worth their time.* From that point on, Ken might stop trying to get anyone's attention. And if he does nothing to change his opinion of *himself,* he will probably grow up feeling second-rate and worthless.

A crystallizing event can come in many forms. It might be a certain look from a spouse that reflects a parent's facial expression you always despised. It could be a shout of rage. It might be a particular tone of voice—sarcastic, flattering, too sweet, or slurred. Any number of things can recall and drive home the emotional pain previously felt, bringing the past into the present and confirming our worst fears about ourselves. For many people, from that moment on, much is lost. Life no longer holds joy, hope, freedom, or any of the other things that give it value. A stronghold has been formed.

THE SPREAD OF PAIN

People who are hurting put a *lot* of effort into reducing their pain. As we saw in the previous chapter, the pain produces fear. We are afraid of other people and, more importantly, of ourselves. Then, before we know it, our fear produces pain. We are afraid we won't be liked, so we cease to like ourselves. We are afraid we won't succeed in life, so we stop trying. Talk about a vicious cycle! What's worse: fear or pain? You tell me. They are always together!

I like to compare the spread of pain to a pinball machine. We're the ball that gets shot into the game of life. It doesn't take long for us to hit some situation that causes pain, so *ping*, we bounce away as quickly as we can. But the force of bouncing off that particular situation hurls us, too hard, into another. *Ping, ping.* More pain. Before we know it, we have no time to stop and think about anything. *Ping, ping, ping.* Our lives become consumed with pain and fear, fear and pain. We don't even have the time or energy to think of how we might be able to stop the pain. All we can do is react and quickly tense up for the next jolt. That's no way to live.

As pain spreads, most people continue their fight or flight responses. And frequently, when one response ceases to be effective, or when it begins to cause too much pain, the person finds a different response. Usually, the new response is no better.

For example, those who withdraw may do OK for a while. However, if they realize that other people seem to have strong, healthy relationships that they are unable to form for themselves, they are likely to feel emotional pain. As a result, withdrawal is their pattern. They may find new ways to withdraw: drinking, numerous sexual involvements, or frequent moving from place to place. When the pain of one response becomes too severe, they can try something else for a while. When that becomes too painful, they just move to the next response.

We naturally feel despair when emotional pain intensifies and spreads to other areas of life. However, this is OK *as long as we eventually take an appropriate action to deal with it.* Only after emotional pain grows and spreads do we realize how out of control we actually are. All along we've thought, *Everybody has problems. This response pattern of mine isn't so bad. I can handle it.* But the truth is, we *can't* handle it. If we could have, we would have gotten rid of it long ago. We would have "put childish ways behind us" as soon as we became adults. Instead, those once pesky habits have become serious problems. And one day the cold hard truth hits us: *I can't handle this problem. It's not getting better; it's getting worse. I have no idea what to do. I no longer have the problem—the problem has me!*

It's not a pleasant discovery. No one likes to admit helplessness. Yet it's better to admit it at this point than to keep ignoring the problems. Freedom from these problems will never occur until we stop trying to avoid them and determine to confront them. Of course, that's always easier said than done.

Somewhere along the way, the things we do to protect ourselves as children become destructive adult patterns which eventually become *strongholds.* They cease to be logical responses to problem situations. They are no longer effective ways to deal with difficult circumstances. Rather, they become bastions of pain and fear from which we cannot break free.

Even though our strongholds stand between us and freedom, we run toward them in times of stress. It's ironic. The very things we once did to keep from being controlled become the things that control us—and they control us mercilessly. We don't want to live with them, yet we don't know how we could ever live without them.

In the next section we'll look at how strongholds take control of and prevent us from finding the freedom we seek. Then we'll discover what we can do to eliminate them. It's not going to be easy, but it's certainly not impossible either. The main requirement is *wanting* to see your strongholds fall, realizing that when they do, you'll have to find another way to live and establish some "new and improved" patterns of behavior.

Exercises for Chapter 5

1. Most people try both fight and flight responses to reduce their pain. But usually one or the other seems to become more dominant. Below are lists of both kinds of responses. Check the methods on both lists that you seem to use most often.

FIGHT RESPONSES

Yelling	Hitting
Pushing	Throwing things
Arguing	Talking back
Not listening	Mocking
Interrupting	

Flight Responses

Walking out	Gambling
Slamming doors	Alcoholism
Closing the door	Drug use
Getting away	Over-exercising
Avoiding eye contact	Television
Cold-shoulder treatment	Music
Joining cults	Reading too much
Joining gangs	Self-mutilation
Finding bad friends	Hurting oneself
Starving	Overeating
Sexual immorality	Fantasizing
Pornography	Rethinking
Rationalizing	Perfectionism

2. Have the characteristics you checked above been true of you since childhood? What is the earliest example of each one you can think of?

3. Put a "W" beside each characteristic you wish were true of you.

4. Put an "R" beside any characteristic you marked in question 1 that you would like to get rid of.

5. Do you know anyone who uses withdrawal as a response pattern? How do you feel when people you care for withdraw from you?

6. Do you know people who are almost always confrontational? How do you feel when dealing with such people?

7. On a scale of one (never) to ten (always), score yourself for the following description "Responding to situations without really thinking about what I'm doing."

8. What are some response patterns you have only recently begun to notice in your life?

CHAPTER 6

A Closer Look at Strongholds

I have a friend who spent much of his early life in the hills of Tennessee. One of his dreaded childhood chores was "chopping thistles." He would wander the hills of his grandparents' farm, hoe in hand, digging up all the thistles he could find. It was hot and hard work, and he could see few results. As far as he could tell, a few weeds were standing before he started, and when he finished they weren't. What was the big deal? Why go to all the trouble of sweat, sunburn, and blistered hands to topple a few weeds?

As an adult looking back, however, he can see the importance of what he did. In that shallow soil with all the limestone underneath, thistles grew where not much else would. In fact, they were quite attractive, with deep purple blooms. But beneath those beautiful blooms were terribly sharp barbs on the leaves that made them treacherous for anyone trying to walk across the hill, as well as for any other plants trying to grow. Also, the thistles spread quickly. If left unchecked, the next year they would grow much thicker. Of course, you could still find a circuitous path through them, but it wouldn't take long before it would be impossible to walk across the hillside without being repeatedly scratched by the razor-like leaves.

Our childhood patterns are not unlike thistles. They don't seem so undesirable at first. Some of them actually seem attractive. We know they are there, and they don't appear to be threatening us, so we don't take action. Then one day, to our surprise, we're unable to move without pain because we've let the problem spread for too long. We need to do some "chopping."

The *presence* of strongholds is destructive enough, but the *spread* of strongholds is even more deadly. It's like cancer. Most people who have cancer could live with it—if it didn't spread. Often it goes unnoticed until it has spread so much it's too late to treat. And while it's never too late to deal with your strongholds, the sooner you begin to do something about them, the easier the job will be.

Some problems can be understood only when examined from several different perspectives. The last chapter described what a stronghold is and what it does. We attempted to understand that the patterns we create as children lose their effectiveness as adults.

In this chapter we will attempt to move from the general observations we have been making to examine some specific strongholds. We will also see why our strongholds seem immune to our efforts to demolish them.

NAMING OUR STRONGHOLDS

Any number of things can become a stronghold. I'd like to give you an overview of several categories of strongholds as well as some specific strongholds within each.

As you read through the following pages, it's important to keep in mind that each of these may or may not be a stronghold in a person's life. In other words, I may have a lustful thought but lust does not become a stronghold until it takes over my thinking. The same is true for fear. Obviously, we all have fears from time to time, but only those whose lives are dominated by fear have a stronghold of fear.

Strongholds are those things which control us—they are compulsions. Compulsions are those behaviors that we regret doing, but continue doing. No matter how negative these behaviors are to us and no matter how we hate them, we still do them.

Depression. Like an iceberg, depression has much more below the surface than is actually showing. Ninety percent of the people I counsel suffer from depression, although they may not even realize it when they come in to see me.

Depression can be physiologically and/or psychologically induced. Not always, but sometimes, depression can become a stronghold. When this is the case, the person consistently has depressed feelings, behaviors, beliefs, and thoughts. Depression can lead to *despair, self-pity, loneliness,* and in severe cases thoughts of *suicide.*

Here's how depression spirals downward. When people constantly feel depressed, they can begin to despair of ever feeling differently. Despair brings a hopelessness and loss of objectivity. People in despair just want to give up; they don't believe anything or anyone can help them. Despair is closely linked to *self-pity*. Self-pity causes people not simply to feel sorry for themselves because of what has happened to them, they feel sorry for themselves because they exist, because they are. Despair and self-pity bring loneliness, which is a sense of alienation and separateness (even though they may have loving and caring people in their lives). When the spiral has reached this level, obsessive thoughts of *suicide* can take root.

Doubt. Doubt, in and of itself, is not destructive. Often it can be used to help people know what they believe and why because they were willing to question what they believed. But when doubt keeps us from trusting God, when it causes us to fear him or a loss of control and an inability to trust him, doubt has established itself as a stronghold in our life. Faith is screened out and spiritual growth is brought to a standstill.

Unbelief is one of the offshoots of doubt. After doubt has drained most of the faith from our lives, we're left not believing much of anything. When we give up on God, we naturally turn to other sources of help and hope—none of which work and so become easy targets for other strongholds. Consequently, we are also likely to feel anger, confusion, instability, and an unsettling lack of peace—all roadblocks to freedom.

Bitterness. This is usually one of the best-disguised strongholds. We can recognize many of the strongholds associated with bitterness, yet we don't always realize we feel bitter. We can identify *resentment* when someone has offended us. We may occasionally express *hate* toward someone who seems particularly evil. And we usually know when *unforgiveness* is in our lives. However, we may not know to what extent some of these things control us.

I have heard people attest, "I'm a good Christian, and I love God with all my heart, but I just cannot forgive that person." But for the Christian, forgiving others isn't an option. It's a command (see Matthew 6:12-15; Colossians 3:13). Our strongholds have the power to distort truth to the extent that we can live a lie and convince ourselves it's not a problem.

Bitterness, if allowed to fester, can become so severe it leads to *violence*. Most of the time people simply think of ways to punish the offender, but they only succeed in punishing themselves with additional emotional pain. Yet in other instances, people act on their feelings and become violent—sometimes against the offending person, and occasionally against themselves. In extreme cases, bitterness leads to murder. Actions taken in "the heat of the moment" are more likely the result of feelings that have been building for much longer.

Most of the time people simply think of ways to punish the offender, but they only succeed in punishing themselves with additional emotional pain.

Anger goes hand-in-hand with bitterness. Anger in itself is not sinful. God is angered when people commit evil actions. When such actions are against *us*, we feel the same righteous anger toward the evil that is done. But we almost always allow our anger to get out of control, and we resort to sinful methods of expression.

It works both ways. Righteous anger can develop into a stronghold. And almost every outburst of what appears to be sinful, out-of-control anger will have at least some degree of righteous anger underneath. We keep telling ourselves we have every right to be angry, which we do, but in the meantime our anger gains more and more control of our lives. For that reason we're urged not to let a day pass without properly dealing with the anger within us (see Ephesians 4:26-27). I also believe it's why Jesus was so quick to equate anger with murder in his Sermon on the Mount (see Matthew 5:21-26).

Rebellion. We usually think of rebellion in negative terms. Yet we also glorify the image of a rebel. We admire people who stand up to bossy leaders or outmoded and stuffy rules and procedures. Why?

For one thing, rebellion in itself is not a problem. Indeed, we often think of rebels as those who fight for freedom. So if we're on a search for freedom, shouldn't we be a bit rebellious?

To rebel against injustice and evil is a good instinct. Yet sometimes the act of rebellion—even rebellion at the right times and for the right reasons—becomes such a thrill that we stop picking our fights and open ourselves up to numerous other strongholds.

We sometimes start becoming rebellious just to have things our own way. Right on the heels of this *self-will* comes the stronghold of *stubbornness*. We can stop being sensitive to the opinions and needs of other people. When we're so busy "looking out for number one," we start building walls around ourselves. Before long, *strife* sets in. We become so stubborn that we can't get along with anyone. Those who tolerate us don't really have the desire to relate with us.

Insecurity. The stronghold of insecurity is tied to fear, which we will deal with last. Insecurity has a myriad of manifestations, each with its own special destructive nature.

Certainly *inferiority* is a stronghold for many people. On a broad scale, most of us seem to have a "them" and "us" mentality. "They" are wealthy, successful, comfortable, talented, lovers of their work, patrons of the arts, and so forth. "We," on the other hand, are inferior. It doesn't matter how accomplished we are. If feelings of inferiority pervade our thoughts, we are never satisfied with ourselves or our life. We think, if I'm an inferior person, how can I ever be adequate to do what my parents, my boss, God, my spouse, or any number of other people expect of me?

Timidity and *shyness* may also be warning signs that a person struggles with feelings of inferiority. We may miss these signals, however, because we write them off as character traits. Or we try to justify our feelings of inferiority by insisting we are simply trying to live the "quiet life" Paul calls us to (see 1 Thessalonians 4:11). If we choose self-control as a spiritual discipline, that's good. A "gentle and quiet spirit" (1 Pt 3:4) is an excellent goal. But when we mask our insecurity by sounding spiritual, we are on the road to developing a stronghold.

Pride. We always lose when we seek to evaluate ourselves against other people. As we have just seen, if we compare and don't like what we see, we feel inferior. But if we compare and convince ourselves that we're better off, we become proud.

Sometimes we take too much credit for the gifts God has given us. The result is an inflated *ego*. Even when we verbally acknowledge God's part, we may put the focus on the wrong area. "I'd like to praise God for *my wonderful singing ability* that I can use for his glory." Other people don't even try to hide their pride but instead bask in sheer *vanity*. "I'm tall, tan, trim, and good looking. What else could anyone ask for?" (A little depth of character, perhaps?)

When inner qualities rather than physical characteristics are at issue, pride can result in *self-righteousness*. The classic example is the Pharisee who dared to pray, "God, I thank you that I am not like other men" (see Luke 18:9-14). Jesus saw through and condemned such self-righteousness. *Self-centeredness* makes pride a difficult problem to deal with. The continual focus on self prevents us from an objective perspective of how distorted our views are. When we cease to care about anyone other than ourselves, we can't see that pride is harmful and destructive. And if we can't see the harm in it, why do anything about it?

Infirmities and addictions. Much of what we have listed has pertained to things which control us emotionally or internally. But frequently our strongholds establish physical control over us as well. Many times people start smoking out of rebellion, only to become addicted to nicotine. Others become alcoholics or drug addicts—to illegal and legal drugs. Still others are addicted to food.

Even people who are free of these classic addictions may be

entangled in a number of other *compulsions:* TV viewing, worry, distorted thinking, reading, talking, and exercise. Even our "nervous habits" can be signals that we need to make some internal adjustments.

Sexual impurity. Many people tend to be judgmental about sexual issues. We discount the fact that many of these activities are highly pleasurable. Later, however, we deal with the remorse, guilt, and other aftereffects of our actions. If we get involved in a recurring sexual behavior we just can't seem to shake, we usually know something is amiss. It is essential that we strive to identify the cause and tend to it. Otherwise, with time, we hate ourselves rather than the sinful actions.

For example, many people become compulsive about pornography or sexual fantasies. Such compulsions won't disappear without help. Guilt and shame build, and can lead to depression and insecurity.

People who decide to identify the source of their lustful feelings may discover that what is missing from their life is actually intimacy, self-esteem, forgiveness, or some other legitimate need. However, when the need isn't met, some try to satisfy it with lustful thoughts that bring an illusion of intimacy. It's much better to conduct an honest examination of one's life and discover the source than to continue with an undesirable behavior, never knowing why we are unable to break free of it and blaming ourselves.

Although Scripture defines sexual sins, they may or may not be a stronghold. Again, strongholds are indicated by compulsive or driven behavior. Strongholds are almost a knee-jerk response to some experience.

Some sexual behaviors not normally considered to be sinful can become strongholds, such as frigidity or the avoidance of sex. In marriage, frigidity becomes a stronghold when the behavior is compulsive. Frigidity can often be traced to childhood experiences, but like any other behavior it can become a stronghold.

Deceit. Most of us don't want to admit our problem to others—and perhaps not even to ourselves. We want to keep our actions secret. So we resort to *lying*—about where we've been, how we feel about our marriage partner, and so much more.

Others *fantasize.* The young woman who keeps seeing a married man frequently creates lavish fantasies about his leaving his wife, sweeping her off her feet, and carrying her away to a lifetime of eternal bliss.

Again *guilt, self-condemnation, shame,* and *unworthiness* accompany these private sins. Deceit is a cruel stronghold. It affects the way we see ourselves. When we are deceived into thinking we are "too bad" to be helped, we become even more vulnerable to the strongholds in our life.

The occult. When we get desperate for answers, we may turn to a source that will tell us what we want to hear.

Involvement in the occult can begin innocently enough at childhood parties or sleep overs. That's where many "good" kids are introduced to Ouija Boards and are told that spirits can help give them guidance and secret wisdom.

Others are introduced to the occult through *astrology.* Rather than enter into a personal relationship with God, they prefer to depend on astrology for guidance about their future and fortune.

In more extreme cases, people become involved with *witchcraft,* where they try to gain power over their fortunes. When they can't find power over the problems in their lives one way, they try to do so in other ways. But spells and potions do not provide the answers they are looking for, and their supernatural involvements become just another problem.

Many people don't take their involvement in the occult very seriously. They don't think anything could possibly be wrong with checking a horoscope or participating in an occasional seance at a party. But God makes himself clear: "Let no one be found among you who sacrifices his son or daughter in the fire, who practices divination or sorcery, interprets omens, engages in witchcraft, or casts spells, or who is a medium or spiritist or who consults the dead. Anyone who does these things is detestable to the Lord" (Dt 18:10-12).

Fears. Much was said about four major fears in chapter four. Each of those fears can become strongholds: *fears of failure, rejection, punishment,* and *feeling shame and other negative emotions.* But we can add other fears to the list as well.

For some people, *phobias* become strongholds. A phobia is a fear of something that isn't logical and can't be explained. People can have phobias about high places, crowded places, bridges, insects—the list is endless.

Self-rejection can turn into a stronghold. We can become so dissatisfied with ourselves that we are unable to be satisfied in our assessments of others. Two other fears that are related to self-rejection are *fear of people* and *fear of not measuring up.* It's possible to have a phobic reaction to being around people. People with this fear simply shut down when they have to face others. The fear of not measuring up causes people to constantly compare themselves with others—and to always come up short. People with this fear hate to do most things because it means they will have to compare and be disappointed with their conclusion.

THE STRONGHOLD COMBO

I'll say it again, one stronghold usually leads to another... and another... and still another. A person could easily have a large number of strongholds. We have no trouble detecting some of them, yet we may remain blind to others. Sometimes strongholds become damaging because we think we have them under control. By the time we discover we actually don't, though, it's too late. They control *us*.

We can be deceived about:

- The existence of strongholds in our lives.
- The rapid growth of any specific stronghold.
- The rapid spread of a network of strongholds as soon as one is firmly established.
- The extent of their destructive power.

I believe this is why David wrote, "Search me, O God, and know my heart; test me and know my anxious thoughts. See if there is any offensive way in me, and lead me in the way everlasting" (Ps 139:23-24). David realized that he couldn't always see the sinful and potentially damaging things in his life. He needed God's help, and so do we.

It is the inhibiting power of the Holy Spirit that keeps our strongholds from having more destructive power over us than they do.

Do you believe that one of the tasks of the Holy Spirit is to convict us of the sin in our lives and to help us understand the gravity of our actions? If so, it should come as no surprise that we need God's help with our strongholds. If we were naturally able to detect them as we should, why would that responsibility be given to the Holy Spirit?

We often receive God's help without recognizing it or giving him credit. It is the inhibiting power of the Holy Spirit that keeps our strongholds from having more destructive power over us than they do. When we feel the pain begin and start to struggle, we need to solicit God's help. That's what Jim did.

Jim is a pastor in his mid-forties. He has been married for sixteen years and has two children. You would never guess that Jim has struggled for years with sexual fantasies. While he has never been physically unfaithful to his wife, he admits, "I've skated close to affairs at times."

He remembers that at age ten or eleven, his normal adolescent curiosity about sex evolved into a vivid fantasy life. As he grew older and discovered pornographic magazines, this seemingly harmless habit grew stronger and stronger until it was no longer manageable. One evening as Jim was driving alone through the city, the Lord began to bring these various incidents of fantasy to his mind, one by one.

For the first time he saw his old, familiar habit from God's perspective—as something destructive and evil that the Lord hated. He realized that this stronghold controlled him. He saw clearly even though he'd asked God to remove the fantasies from his life, he hadn't really meant it. He had wanted to reserve the option to return to them again. Now he realized he must let go of his improper sexual thoughts for good—to let God take them away and help him never want them back.

God honored Jim's desire. As each individual incident was brought to his mind, Jim confessed it and then rejected it as the sin that God said it was. He thanked God for forgiveness and then determined to keep his mind filled with thankfulness rather than destructive fantasies. That evening he reclaimed the ground he had given up long ago. Since then, Jim hasn't been obsessed with his old fantasies. Not that he is no longer tempted. He is. But, when the thoughts recur, they no longer hold power over him. He knows how to defeat them. He praises God that he no longer has to think such thoughts, and he sets his mind on good things that are worthy of praise. He is no longer enslaved.

Harry also learned that with God's help he could discover freedom from his strongholds. Harry was a multimillionaire with life seemingly under control. However, his apparently happy marriage was being threatened by homosexual undercurrents. A recent shocking event had brought Harry to counseling: he had molested a thirteen-year-old boy. This was an isolated instance that had left Harry ashamed—and scared to death.

As a small boy, Harry had been molested by some of his teenage uncles. The emotional pain and shame were devastating. Through the years, his thoughts frequently were filled with the homosexual acts he had suffered. These thoughts continued to occur even after he got married.

Harry eventually began to believe that he had no choice, and no hope of change. He started to think, *I guess this is just the way I am. I'll never be free of these homosexual thoughts.* But he was so shaken after his abuse of this young boy, a neighbor, that he was at last willing to deal with the problem.

It took a while, but with God's help and commitment to counseling, Harry began to absorb the truth that God loves him and desires the best for him. His life began to change. He saw that shame and anger had ruled him since his own childhood abuse, so he confessed his sin and forgave those who had victimized him years before. Eventually, he worked through his unforgiveness toward his abusers, and he courageously took responsibility for his own abusive actions toward his young neighbor. He resolved the pain and turmoil of his past. For the first time, Harry began to experience freedom from his obsessive homosexual thoughts. Today he and his wife are working together to rebuild and nourish their relationship.

NOW IS THE TIME TO ACT

You can probably recall times when the Holy Spirit suddenly convicted you of a sinful behavior. With the help of the Holy Spirit, perhaps you did something about it. And maybe now you realize that it's time to look back across your life again—a little closer this time.

Jim and Harry both came to a turning point. They discovered they must either get God's help to rid themselves of their strongholds or continue to live with them. Suppose Jim had decided to keep living with his fantasies. His human nature would have made every attempt to justify his behavior: *So I have sexual thoughts that other people don't seem to approve of. Big deal. It's my life and my choice. That's just who I am.*

But had he chosen to give in to the problem, it would have escalated. His defenses would have gone down. The walls of the stronghold would have gotten taller, deeper, and thicker. His sexual thoughts would have become more frequent and intense. His fantasies would continue, but now guilt would be along for the ride.

Anytime we ignore the Holy Spirit's prompting us to deal with sin, the problem gets more entrenched. A woman who struggles with her hot temper might think, *It's just the way I am. Some women are patient and loving. Others are quick-tempered.* As soon as she gives herself over to the problem, the stronghold intensifies. A teenage boy hears all the facts about drug use. After a little experimentation and initial reluctance, he makes his choice: *I just enjoy getting high. That's all. I'm not doing anyone any harm, and I can quit whenever I want to.* Later, when he *does* try to quit, the stronghold is standing there, preventing him from reaching the freedom he now desires.

The more we resist dealing with our strongholds, the more powerful they become. Now is the time to act.

SEEING MORE CLEARLY

It's usually easier to detect other people's strongholds than recognize our own. You can see the wrong ways that other people try to deal with their pain: anger, hatred, addictions, or workaholic tendencies. Too bad we aren't as good at self-evaluation. We delude ourselves.

We need to deal honestly with ourselves. Most people finally ask: "Isn't there something better I can look forward to in life? Can't I get beyond this point?"

The answer to both questions is yes, of course. If you're ready to begin an honest evaluation, here are some questions to ask yourself:

- What kind of life do you think God *wants* you to have?
- What things are keeping you from living the life you have just described?
- What things are you substituting for the life you think God wants for you?
- If you could start living a life of freedom from this minute on, would you be willing to give up all the things you've been substituting? Or would you need to think about it?
- Do you have any fears as you anticipate a change from a life filled with strongholds to a life of freedom?

Most of us, if we're honest, admit that we feel fear when it comes to change of *any* kind. We've learned to cope, so we settle for coping rather than living in freedom. It's ironic. We want things to be different in our lives, but we are afraid to change.

If this is the way you feel, don't think you're strange. It's one of the major obstacles that must be overcome before strongholds can be demolished for good.

It will do little good, however, if you try to change before you see where you stand and how you operate. A person on the top floor of a three-story building usually doesn't want to jump out the window. But if the building catches fire and the only escape is out the window, most people become a lot less reluctant to risk change—especially if some supportive people are on the ground holding a net.

In the following chapters, I hope to light a fire underneath you to encourage you to jump. But I will also have the safety net ready. Jump to freedom and let your strongholds burn behind you. Flying through the air will be a little scary. But when you get up and walk away—and you will—you'll walk away free.

Exercises for Chapter 6

1. The following list illustrates some strongholds common to many people. Place a score next to each one, based on the following scale:

   0 - Not present in my life at all

   1 - Is a small problem for me

   2 - Is more than a small problem for me

   3 - Makes my life miserable

AREAS OF STRONGHOLDS

DEPRESSION
Despair
Self-pity
Loneliness
Suicide

DOUBT
Unbelief

BITTERNESS
Resentment
Hate
Unforgiveness
Violence
Anger (sinful)
Murder

REBELLION
Self-will
Stubbornness
Strife

INSECURITY
Inferiority
Inadequacy
Timidity
Shyness

PRIDE
Ego
Vanity
Self-righteousness
Self-centeredness

ADDICTIONS
Compulsions
Nicotine
Alcoholism
Drug involvement
Food

SEXUAL IMPURITY
Lust
Masturbation
Homosexuality
Adultery
Fornication
Frigidity

DECEIT
Lying
Fantasizing
Guilt
Self-condemnation
Shame
Unworthiness

OCCULT
Ouija Board
Astrology
Witchcraft
Sects
Religion

FEARS
Phobias
Rejection
Failure
Punishment
Feelings of shame
Self-rejection
Fear of people
Fear of not measuring up
Indecision
Perfectionism
Denial

2. How can you prevent problems in these areas from growing from a 1 to a 3?

3. We have said that God may allow a stronghold to dominate our lives in order to motivate us to do something about it rather than continuing to feel miserable. Can you think of examples of this from your own past? Can you think of any ways this might be happening to you right now?

CHAPTER 7

Messages from the Past; Help for the Present

—▲—

Y ou're cruising down a stretch of busy interstate, making good time, when suddenly your car conks out. You narrowly avoid getting hit as you coast to the side of the road. You can't get your car started, so what do you do? I see three primary options: (1) If you don't know a crankcase from a suitcase, you probably wait or call someone for help. (2) If you know your way around an engine, you pop the hood, see what's wrong, make the necessary adjustments, and once more go on your way. (3) Even if you're a skilled mechanic, you may see that the problem will require more than you can do right at that minute—a new part, a tool you don't have with you, or some other need—so you would seek emergency help.

When it comes to dealing with strongholds, our options are not much different. Some of us have been stranded on the roadside of life for years, waiting for help. We don't know how to fix what is wrong, but we can't move on until we do. Others of us have been able to recognize some of the problems and fix them, which has allowed us to get a little farther down the road. But most of us, even those of us who have a lot of experience and knowledge, eventually are stalled by a problem.

So far this book has dealt primarily with the first two levels: identifying specific problems and affirming that most of us need help with them. From here on we move into the third category: discovering what it takes to repair the problems we can't handle on our own.

GET THE MESSAGE?

Certain messages reinforce our strongholds. Whoever said "Sticks and stones can break my bones, but words can never hurt me" was dead wrong. In fact, words stick with us far longer than it takes any bruise to heal.

Frances was a troubled thirty-three-year-old woman with a sad history of shallow sexual involvements with a succession of men. Drugs provided a way for her to forget her emotional pain, at least for a while. As we talked, she told me that ever since she was a little girl she had always believed there was something evil about her. Her belief caused her to distance herself from other children.

Frances recalled that when she was four years old she was traumatized by an event between herself and her mother. Frances' mother took pride in their lovely home and worked hard to keep everything neat and pretty. Whenever Mom would have a bad day, France's would draw and color pictures to cheer her up.

One day her mother had been working extremely hard, so that afternoon Frances presented one of her works of art. The praise and compliments she received so excited the little artist that she accidentally wet herself, making a puddle on the freshly waxed floor. Her mother, exhausted by this time, lost control. It was an unusual, isolated event, but her mother shouted some things that burned into her daughter's mind. One of those phrases really stung: "You are evil."

Frances never forgot those words. More importantly, she began to believe that they were true, even though her mother hadn't meant what she said. The mother had long forgotten what she had said. But as the years passed, Frances began to act out her belief about herself through promiscuity and drug use. Her life was filled with depression, pain, and intense anger.

Frances finally learned to believe God's opinion of her rather than the faulty one she had formed about herself. She confronted the lies she had embraced for so long and agreed with God that they were wrong. After confessing her own sin, she forgave her mother for the terrible words that had been spoken. When I last saw Frances, she had a completely new countenance, beaming with hope and freedom.

Messages define our lives. If we could look at a list of messages, both verbal and nonverbal, that a person had received, especially the early childhood messages, we could guess with significant accuracy what kind of life the person was presently experiencing.

For example, some messages are verbal labels. Consider the following words and phrases:

Pitiful	Loser
Liar	Never amount to anything
Lazy	Stupid
Incompetent	No one would ever want you
Failure	Freak
Worthless	

Other messages are nonverbal, conveyed through looks that communicate as clearly as any speech ever written. See if you can remember looks that instantly transferred the following emotions or messages to you:

Disgust	Hatred
You're inferior	You don't exist
Exasperation	Impatience
Blame	I'm surprised at you
Accusation	Indifference
Prudishness	Distaste
Frustration	Disbelief
Suspicion	Anger
Arrogance	Disapproval
Shock	Boredom
Jealousy	Grumpiness
Obstinance	Rage

Sometimes nonverbal behavior takes the form of a series of actions. Nonverbal behavior can in some ways cause more difficulty than straightforward verbal messages. And children cannot readily defend themselves against a harsh tactic used by many parents: mixing negative nonverbal messages with neutral or positive verbal communication. Even adults have problems seeing through this emotional fraud—as Alice and Doc's experience reveals.

Nonverbal behavior can in some ways cause more difficulty than straightforward verbal messages.

Alice had been with Doc through all his long days of medical school and internship. They had married young, so she had worked long hours, both at a job and in their home, to take as much of the load off her husband as she could. Along the way she had lost some of her natural sparkle and gained a little extra weight. But they had made it! He had become a specialist who was making more money than they had ever dreamed of. Alice no longer had to go to a job she dreaded. Now she could relax and benefit from some of her hard work. At least, she thought she could.

But to Alice's dismay, Doc almost immediately took up with another woman who was younger, sexier, and free of the signs of wear and tear that Alice had. When she came to me, Alice was trying to win back her husband by letting him off easy. Based on some of her comments, however, I suspected that this might have been his plan all along. It didn't really matter whether he had planned it or not. Just the thought that he had used her all these years was maddening. I referred Alice to the most aggressive lawyer I know. Note that Alice's husband may not have said anything negative, but his behavior communicated negative things to her. She believed she was just there to be used by him.

AS A PERSON THINKETH...

Try to think of some of the negative messages you tell yourself about yourself. Many times these are messages you received from other people but are now repeating. Why do we curse each other and then ourselves in this way?

Sometimes misguided parents think that if they can make their children feel badly enough about themselves, then they will behave as the parents want them to. They do not realize that we act the way we do, not because of how badly we feel but because of what we believe to be true about ourselves. Someone who thinks she is stupid will act stupidly no matter how bright she really is. If you tell your son he is a no-good loser, then be prepared to see him get in all kinds of trouble.

Sometimes parents use labels to retaliate after the child has hurt or disappointed them in some way. The extent of the damage may never be detected, however. Words leave no physical marks, but their harmful impact can last for a lifetime.

Sometimes misguided parents think that if they can make their children feel badly enough about themselves, then they will behave as the parents want them to.

Lydia, for example, was exhausted and tearful as she poured out her story. She is a young woman with so many projects she can hardly count them. A missing button on her jacket is a silent testimony to her disorganized life and the difficulty of coping with the demands on her. Her life is filled with endless details she would rather not think about: two children, a husband, church responsibilities, and a full-time job.

I wondered how any human being could expect to do justice to so many responsibilities. After listening to the remarkable schedule Lydia tries to maintain, I began to ask some questions about her background. She said she had grown up in a home with only herself, an older sister, and a widowed father. Her mother had died a few months after Lydia's birth, after which the father had devoted his energies to his two daughters.

When the father realized he couldn't be both mother and father to the girls, he had enlisted the help of his sister, Margaret. Aunt Margaret, trying to cope with two active youngsters, found that a sharp tongue would usually achieve the goals she wanted. She frequently scolded and cautioned the girls—especially Lydia, who was younger—against trying new things that might prove too difficult for them. At the same time, Aunt Margaret excelled in a number of areas. Among other things, she was known as an excellent cook, seamstress, and keeper of a prize-winning flower and vegetable garden.

Somehow the combination of Aunt Margaret's personal achievements and her low expectations, fault-finding, and lack of confidence toward the girls left Lydia frozen with indecision. She would wait until the last minute to do homework or household duties, and then would discover she was not completely satisfied with her hurried results. To make matters more dismal, Lydia had to endure the angry comments of her aunt. After Lydia married and began her family, she found new areas of commitment, but the same poor habits that had troubled her for so long seemed much more serious now. She became more mired down with each passing year. Finally, she decided to look for some direction and help.

If the only time you are accepted is when you perform up to a certain standard, then *you are never accepted*. Only your performance is found acceptable.

As we continued to meet, Lydia began to recall specific false messages she had received and believed from well-meaning Aunt Margaret. Most of these messages pertained to Lydia's inability to competently plan and pursue a task to its completion. As this became clear to the adult Lydia, she discovered she still harbored significant unforgiveness and bitterness toward her aunt. After confessing her feelings to her heavenly Father, Lydia experienced much resolution and was eager to ask her aunt's forgiveness.

They met, and Lydia gently explored the subject but was disappointed to discover that Aunt Margaret remembered things much differently. In fact, Margaret didn't seem to have any idea what

Lydia meant as she spoke of the difficulties she had experienced. Lydia found it necessary to leave the situation as it was, having done everything in her power to make it right. Her confession and the forgiveness she extended to Aunt Margaret were sufficient to enable her to begin replacing the faulty old opinions of herself with the truth that she was indeed capable of making good decisions and carrying through with her plans. She got a late start, learning in her middle adult years what many discover in childhood. However, she is glad to be making progress with the encouragement of God's Word.

Conditional acceptance by other people sends powerful messages to anyone but especially to children. Many people grow up feeling accepted only after they have performed well enough. Think about the message that is being sent. If the only time you are accepted is when you perform up to a certain standard, then *you are never accepted*. Only your performance is found acceptable. When this happens, especially when it comes from someone you've trusted, the message is, "You have no worth except to be used."

People who have been physically and sexually abused can usually recall negative messages they received, perhaps years ago, that continue to haunt them. Jeanie was the wife of an extremely successful businessman who beat her. His abuse had been going on more than fifteen years. When I asked Jeanie what was the most difficult part of her experience, she answered immediately: "It was the disgust in his eyes." Messages can be carved so deeply within the soul of their target that the person continues to repeat them long after the offending person has been left in the past.

Many people in our culture promote the philosophy that once a victim, always a victim. What I'm saying may sound harsh to someone who agrees with that philosophy. But the truth is that we become our own worst enemy as we believe the words of those who have hurt us so badly and continue to give those messages our time and attention. We are living proof of how powerful they are.

LEAVING IT BEHIND

I believe strongholds *can* be demolished. We need not remain victims all our lives. We can do something to change and to turn our lives around.

Earlier I defined a stronghold as "any area of our lives we cannot control which is destructive." Until our strongholds are identified and addressed, we will never be the people we ought to (and want to) be. Our problems continue, however, because we never *see* what we're doing wrong, so our strongholds continue to destroy us and the people around us.

Maybe you've tried all kinds of things in the past, only to see your strongholds still standing, becoming stronger and stronger. Don't give up. They *can* be destroyed. Regardless of the strangle-hold it's had on you in the past, it will cease to be important once you deal with it.

I say this to contrast this method with someone who uses a cold-turkey approach to stop smoking. You may know people who seem to dwell on smoking more after they *stop* than while they were smokers. Even after they quit, it remains a major issue (and perhaps a sore point) for them. But once you successfully demolish a stronghold, you'll be able to take a deep breath and get on with your life without wanting to look back. You will be able to look at events in the past objectively: "That happened to me. It was terrible. But now I can go on, leaving it behind."

By now you should understand the problems associated with strongholds. You should be relating to the helpless feelings shared by everyone else who has strongholds. And, I hope, you're ready to do whatever it takes to demolish the strongholds in your own life. If you need to do some additional thinking or analyzing of the material we've already covered, now is the time to do it. From this point on, we're going to be dealing with solutions to the problem.

NOT A DO-IT-YOURSELF PROJECT

Simply put, strongholds are spiritual problems that require a spiritual solution. I realize that by introducing the spiritual element to the problems you're facing, I am opening myself up for misinterpretation. If so, we need to deal with your questions before moving on. Whenever I meet with people to discuss strongholds, some of the questions almost everyone asks are:

- "Why haven't I ever been able to find someone to love me just the way I am?"
- "If God loved me, why would he allow me to have such powerful strongholds?"
- "If God truly loves me, why doesn't he stop my pain and confusion?"
- "Why did God create me with all these problems?"

As people struggle with these questions, many come to wrong assumptions about God. They accuse him of all kinds of things. They challenge his creative design by wishing they were someone else. They lose hope by feeling that *if God created me this way, I can never expect to be anything but miserable*. They feel he is using them as pawns in some sort of cosmic game. People who have been physically or sexually abused often conclude that God created them for the purpose of being abused. They see no other possible reason for their existence. They think, *Apparently God never cared for me, so he created me with this lot in life.*

We've been talking about the search for freedom, but these people have ceased to consider freedom as one of their options. They are hurting too badly. What they don't realize is that God is hurting too. God is grieved when we don't accept the freedom he provided on the cross. The whole purpose of Jesus' sacrificial death was so we could "cast all [our] anxiety on him because he cares for [us]" (1 Pt 5:7).

Yes, life is unfair. Yes, we may suffer pain and fear as the result of evil in the world—indeed, as a result of the evil in our own lives. However, what we must do to find healing and freedom is to confront the evil. We're too good at hiding what isn't here, so *we must allow God to expose it.* This is never easy. But we're incapable of dealing with such a powerful problem in our own strength.

We may have already prayed for God to eliminate our strongholds, especially the more obvious ones such as anger and depression. When the strongholds aren't immediately destroyed, we assume God answers other people's prayers and not ours. But perhaps God actually wants us to discover that he has provided us what it takes to deal with the problem. We have his Holy Spirit, access to his power and authority, promises from Scripture, and much more. Yet sometimes we are tricked into sitting passively, waiting for God to do every little thing for us, and feeling defeated. We need to learn to take action when action is called for. *Passivity is the Christian's worst problem.*

An analogy I like to use is of the 1991 war in the Persian Gulf. Saddam Hussein invaded Kuwait. Though he was directly responsible for the invasion, he did not take part personally. His army "claimed" Kuwait, but that did not make the small country his. Kuwait still belonged to Kuwait, but Hussein had established a stronghold there. The only way to have him removed was through warfare. A coalition of forces had to overpower his army, who had no right to be there. Hussein's stronghold had to be destroyed. And now, even though Hussein has withdrawn his troops, Kuwait must stand watch and ensure he doesn't return and do it all over again.

Sometimes we are tricked into sitting passively,
waiting for God to do every little thing for us,
and feeling defeated. We need to learn
to take action.

Satan does all he can to establish a stronghold in your life, but God has given his people the power and authority to demolish those strongholds and run him out. Our lives belong to God, but Satan can boldly lay claim to them even though he has no right to do so.

We need to identify evil. Many methods for dealing with strongholds are evil because they miss God's mark for us. We need to start over. We need to closely examine our patterns and strongholds, and consciously decide to handle our problems God's way.

Below is a prayer I recommend to people who are plagued with destructive messages from their past. If you struggle with unhealthy thoughts, perhaps this prayer will be helpful to you. (I suggest you pray aloud.)

PRAYER FOR DEALING WITH NEGATIVE THOUGHTS

Dear Lord,

I have been believing the negative thought of (*name the thought.*) I hate thinking this thought. This thought is not a healthy one for me. It is against what you want me to think. I want to bring my thoughts into obedience to your thoughts.

For though we live in the world, we do not wage war as the world does. The weapons we fight with are not the weapons of the world. On the contrary, they have divine power to demolish strongholds. We demolish arguments and every pretension that sets itself up against the knowledge of God, and we take captive every thought to make it obedient to Christ.

2 Corinthians 10:3-5

I also want to think about things that are worthy of praise.

Whatever is true, whatever is noble, whatever is right, whatever is pure, whatever is lovely, whatever is admirable—if anything is excellent or praiseworthy—think about such things.

Philippians 4:8

Thank you for forgiving me, for accepting this thought that has affected my life so negatively. I now, by my own free will, choose to replace the negative thought of (*name the thought*) with what you want me to think. The next time I think that negative thought, help me to tell you and change it.

Thank you for the truth that sets me free.

WHO WILL RESCUE ME?

In order to eliminate the destructive patterns of behavior that dominate our struggle for freedom, we need to identify the whereabouts of the strongholds we face. The Scriptures teach us to choose to live by the Spirit (see Galatians 5:16-18). Admittedly, the

Spirit of God dwelling within our spirit is in opposition to the ungodly thinking and feeling processes dominating our lives. Yet God allows each man and woman to choose our deepest beliefs about ourselves, about him, and about each other.

Our strongholds are located in the deepest feeling and thinking processes of our soul. We know we've been saved. We know we're supposed to have love, joy, peace, freedom, and all the other things God promises. But we just can't shake our strongholds, the baggage of a lifetime of rejection and failure. We use the best of our fleshly tactics to combat them, but nothing works. We might accuse God of not loving us enough to rid us of our ongoing problems. We can mourn with Paul: "What a wretched man I am! Who will rescue me from this body of death?" (Rom 7:24).

But God does love us enough. His intention is that we replace our old sinful behaviors with the new behaviors of a free person. He can see what we cannot: that once our lives are filled with love, joy, peace, and the like, we will be more content and much better off. The search for freedom is impeded until we stop "doing what comes naturally" and start listening to and obeying God's Spirit. "Those who belong to Christ Jesus have crucified the sinful nature with its passions and desires. Since we live by the Spirit, let us keep in step with the Spirit. Let us not become conceited, provoking and envying one another" (Gal 5:24-26).

We must choose God's way over our way. And while it sounds simple to choose God, it's not easy. The Bible describes the process of getting rid of our old, familiar sinful ways as crucifixion. And even though salvation was a one-time event, keeping in step with the Spirit is a day-by-day, minute-by-minute challenge.

This is where the soul comes into play. The soul functions as the psychical nature of man. The Greeks used the word *psuche* (commonly psyche) to describe the relationship of our spirit to our ability to think, feel, and choose. These soul functions, in a sense, are caught in the middle of a war between our old lives and the associated destructive patterns of thinking, feeling, and choosing, and the regenerated spirit of the new birth. It's where the battle ensues between our old ways and God's better way. The condition of the soul can be influenced by many things: our old fleshly patterns, the deceit of the devil, and the truth of God. But a Christian whose spirit is indwelt by the Holy Spirit can choose which influences to respond to.

The contrast between the soul and spirit is divisible only by God's Holy Spirit: "For the word of God is living and active and sharper than any two-edged sword, and piercing as far as the division of soul and spirit" (Heb 4:12, NAS), but it can be influenced by the desires of our hearts: "But if from there you seek the Lord your God, you will find him if you look for him with all your heart and with all your soul" (Dt 4:29); "Create in me a pure heart, O God, and renew a steadfast spirit within me" (Ps 51:10); "And he who searches our hearts knows the mind of the Spirit, because the Spirit intercedes for the saints in accordance with God's will" (Rom 8:27).

God gives us the choice to keep in step with the Spirit so that our old fleshly patterns will not automatically take over. If we listen to the messages of our old lives, we will continue to live in pain and bondage. And while there is a degree of pain involved in breaking free, the genuine freedom that results is worth any price.

God sent the Holy Spirit to help us appropriate the freedom only he can provide for our souls. Don't give up now. But don't go rushing ahead, either! Spend some time in this chapter, in prayer, and in meditation. It's a lot to take in during one sitting—especially if it's new to you. You may have a lot of questions; that's OK. If so, write them down and find someone you trust who can help you think through them.

Exercises for Chapter 7

1. Some of the messages we tell ourselves can be identified through simple sentence completion. Finish each of the following sentences with the first thoughts that come to your mind.

   • Mom would have liked me more if I had...

   • Dad would have liked me more if I had...

   • Other people would like me more if I would...

   • The one thing that might have made us a better family would have been...

   • I frequently catch myself thinking about my childhood when I...

   • The times I tend to feel "like such a terrible person" are when...

2. As you reflect on how you completed the previous sentences, what messages do you think might be ingrained into your thinking patterns? (For any that come to mind, have you prayed the "Prayer for Dealing with Negative Thoughts Prayer" on page 128?)

3. Which of the following labels are you most sensitive to?
    (Check all that apply.)

Pitiful	Loser
Liar	Never amount to anything
Lazy	Stupid
Incompetent	No one would ever want you
Failure	Freak
Worthless	

4. Of the following looks, mark with a "C" the ones you were
    most sensitive to as a child. Then go back through the list and
    mark with an "A" the ones you still dread as an adult.

Disgust	Hatred
"You're inferior"	"You don't exist"
Exasperation	Impatience
Blame	"I'm surprised at you"
Accusation	Indifference
Prudishness	Distaste
Frustration	Disbelief
Suspicion	Anger
Arrogance	Disapproval
Shock	Boredom
Jealousy	Rage
Grumpiness	Obstinance

5. It is the Holy Spirit working in a person's spirit that keeps the
    soul and body under control so the person can be free. When
    strong desires and demands come from the soul or body, how
    do you think it affects the person's attempt to keep in step with
    the Spirit?

6. Below are several circumstances representing the impact of the Holy Spirit on our thinking and feeling processes. For each situation, choose a percentage corresponding to the influence of your old sinful nature. The remainder represents the influence of the Holy Spirit through your own spirit. The resulting diagram will illustrate the areas of your life where you are still struggling with strongholds.

   In prayer, ask the Lord to reveal these areas to you, that you might be able to yield those influences to the Holy Spirit.

   During the following circumstances and in your most recent experiences, how much would you say you allowed yourself to be led by your emotions, your mind, or the Holy Spirit.

EXAMPLE

Situation I: Relationship to my boss:

MIND	EMOTIONS	LED BY THE HOLY SPIRIT
<—I—>	<—I—>	<—I—>
30%	70%	0%
(30% of my thought processes dominated by my sinful nature)	(70% of my thought processes dominated by my sinful nature)	(0% of my thought processes are Spirit-controlled)

PRAYER

I have not entirely abandoned my rights as an employee. I judge my worth by my supervisor's approval, feeling rejection and failure. Lord, please guide my thoughts and feelings by the power of the Holy Spirit, and illuminate to me my worth in Jesus Christ.

	MIND	EMOTIONS	LED BY THE HOLY SPIRIT
Situation I	<————>	<————>	<————>
Situation II	<————>	<————>	<————>
Situation III	<————>	<————>	<————>
Situation IV	<————>	<————>	<————>

CHAPTER 8

Getting to the Root
of the Problem

O ne spring when I was growing up in Oklahoma, the dandelions on our property were completely out of control. My dad thought dandelion removal would be a good job for me, and he instructed me to dig them up by the roots. So that's what I started doing. But a teenager can think of a lot of ways to spend his time on a beautiful, sunny day, so I devised a shortcut. I brilliantly figured out that the only part of the dandelions that showed were the yellow tops. It was quicker to lop off the tops with a sweep of the hoe than to dig down and get to the roots of every one of those pesky weeds.

With my innovative approach to the problem, I was done in no time and free to pursue more worthwhile interests. But you know what happened, don't you? Sure enough, in less than a week I was spending another beautiful, sunny day with my hoe, this time digging up the weeds by their roots. It had taken no time for the dandelions, still firmly rooted in the soil, to produce new blooms. I could have gone out every few days to chop off the tops. But each time I did, I would only have been creating more work for myself. I was a fast learner, so the second time I wanted to do the job right and get it over with, once and for all.

It's too bad I wasn't such a quick learner when it came to emotional patterns. I kept repeating the same mistakes over and over. And I suspect that many other people keep avoiding the real work required to get rid of their problems. It seems much easier to attend to the cosmetic part of the problem—the part that shows itself. We take what we think is the path of least resistance, and we do it again and again... and again... and again.

Our response patterns kick into gear and we keep using ineffective methods as the problem grows worse and worse. Regardless of the discomfort, we must learn to dig down deep and get to the root.

We discovered in the previous chapter that our strongholds are located in the soul. They affect us at all levels—mind, will, emotions, thoughts, decisions, and feelings. They are the fortresses that Satan has established to claim territory in our lives. The process has gone something like this:

1. We feel pain from some circumstance, and our flesh wants to do something to reduce the pain.

2. Satan energizes our fleshly desires, playing on our craving to feel good.

3. We act to eliminate the pain, using whatever (fleshly) response we can think of to feel better. Eventually we discover that what we are doing is wrong, but we still have an intense desire to feel good.

4. We begin to identify *what we do* (our sinful responses) with *who we are*. We start to think, *I'm such a terrible person.* We hate ourselves rather than merely hating our behavior.

No wonder freedom seems so distant for so many of us. Not only do we suspect that freedom is out of our reach, we are deceived into thinking we don't deserve it! And regardless of the assumptions we are making, breaking this cycle seems too high a price to pay. We are too tired to commit to doing that much work.

What we don't realize is how hard we're *already* working just to keep our level of emotional pain at a manageable level. We need to see how much better it would be to pay a price—any price—to receive the freedom that Jesus has promised is possible. But I suspect if you've read this far, you're at that point. So let's see what we can do about digging up some roots.

A COMMON BOND

As you have seen, strongholds affect our emotions, our fears, our state of mind, our pursuit of pleasure, and essentially every area of our lives. So take another look at your own list of strongholds (page 115) and do a bit of analysis. Up till now you have been focusing on the kinds of strongholds, noting primarily their diversity. But now can you identify anything that all of them have in common?

I believe that bitterness is the root of most of our strongholds. Consider the advice of Hebrews 12:15: "See to it that no one misses the grace of God and that no bitter root grows up to cause trouble and defile many." Whether you struggle with depression, doubt, rebellion, pride, fear, or sexual impurity, or something else, I suspect that underneath the problem is a "bitter root."

When we are bitter, we are unwilling to forgive. Unforgiveness is the part of the problem we're aware of—the bloom—so to speak. We are usually unwilling or unable to forgive those who have hurt us—or to forgive ourselves for becoming a victim. And though we us—or to forgive ourselves for becoming a victim. And though we recognize and try to deal with our unwillingness to forgive, we never deal with our bitterness. We don't get to the root of the problem.

How many times have you decided to forgive someone, only to continue holding the person accountable for the offense? You want to forgive the person (to make yourself feel better, if for no other reason), but you just can't do it. It's like my dandelions. You try to forgive, you follow all the steps prescribed by an author or speaker but you ignore the real problem: your bitterness. It never goes away.

If you struggle with the issue of unforgiveness without doing anything about your underlying bitterness, the problem is sure to pop up again. Bitterness produces unforgiveness.

PAIN (from an offense) —————— BITTERNESS —————UNFORGIVENESS

Christ died to forgive us so we could be free to forgive others. But you can't forgive without first resolving any bitterness.

AN UNCOMMON SOLUTION

This is the key in your search for freedom. If you can destroy the stronghold of bitterness, *then* you can deal with the unforgiveness in your life. Bitterness makes a person extremely vulnerable to unwise decisions and destructive patterns of living. It is as though a shadow stretches across your life or a virus infiltrates your body. This malignancy of the soul is destroyed only as we recognize the reality of its existence and destructiveness. Only then will we plead through prayer to be released. Only then will we truly hate this evil within our souls.

When we are no longer bitter, our forgiveness can become sincere and lasting. And before we know it, our other strongholds start toppling like dominoes. But unless we take out the bitter root, our other strongholds will remain intact and immovable.

So how do we deal with bitterness? In Matthew 18:21-35, Jesus tells a simple story of a man who had been forgiven of an immense debt he could not possibly pay. Soon after receiving such mercy, the man had the opportunity to forgive a small debt against him—an insignificant sum in light of what he himself had been forgiven. Yet he refused to do so! Even though someone else had extended him freedom rather than prison by forgiving a debt, he still planned to imprison another person. He wasn't thankful enough for his own forgiveness to forgive another. One of the most terrifying verses in Scripture is found at the end of this account as Jesus warns us that the heavenly Father will see to it that we encounter torment until we learn to show forgiveness from our hearts.

But how do we learn to forgive from the heart? Look closely at the passage and try to determine your own answer. How can a person experience being let off the hook for a terrible debt—one that would have put him and his entire family into slavery—and then not have the graciousness to forgive another of a small debt? I've asked several groups this question and have received the following possible explanations:

- Perhaps he didn't think he was responsible for the debt he was forgiven.
- Perhaps although he had been forgiven this debt, he then decided to try to raise enough money on his own to pay it off anyway. Then he wouldn't feel indebted to the king's graciousness.
- Perhaps he didn't believe the king.
- Perhaps forgiveness is an unnatural act.

But consider what Jesus was really asking: How can those who receive forgiveness for their own sins—thus avoiding the penalty for those sins, escaping an eternity in hell, and receiving eternal life in heaven—how can they possibly be so thankless and ungrateful as to refuse to forgive other people from their hearts?

Most of us never come close to comprehending what God has done for us. Consequently, we don't come close to extending the forgiveness we should show to others. And to be sure, others may not ask for or deserve our forgiveness, but then, we didn't deserve the forgiveness *we* received.

We deserve judgment but, because of Christ, receive freedom instead. And we are expected to extend the same forgiveness to others as we are able. We are able to forgive others as we begin to see what Jesus really did on the cross for us. The more clearly we understand, the more we love him. And the more we love him, the easier it will become for us to address our bitterness and start to become more forgiving people. This sample prayer may be helpful.

> Heavenly Father,
>
> I have bitterness and unforgiveness in my soul toward *(person's name)* because *(name what that person did)*. I confess that bitterness and unforgiveness are evil in my soul and I hate them. Thank you for forgiving me. I now choose to forgive *(person's name)* for *(name what that person did)*. The next time I remember *(person's name)*, help me remember them as forgiven.
>
> For as you have written: "In this is love, not that we loved God, but that He loved us and sent His only begotten Son to be the propitiation for our sins" (1 John 4:10, NAS).

Don't get me wrong. We don't change overnight. As we saw in the last chapter, strongholds are in our soul, and the soul is a battleground where Satan exerts his destructive influence.

But when you eliminate bitterness, you *will* see results. If you dig up that evil root, you will experience the first glimpse of true freedom you've had in a long time.

ARE YOU WILLING TO LET GO?

Before we discuss the process for destroying strongholds, I have a few questions for you: Do you really want to demolish your strongholds? Are you willing to risk freedom in place of the familiar patterns you now have?

These questions are not easy. To someone who is genuinely free, the answers seem obvious. But if you've tolerated a number of strongholds, you know it seems impossible to live without them. In some situations it's much more comfortable to be a slave; at least you always know what to expect.

Strongholds grow in power in two basic ways: *denial* and *deflection*.

Denial manifests itself in three ways.

1. *Problem? What Problem?* Some people simply refuse to admit that they have any kind of problems. So the more severe the problem, the firmer the denial. I know I've certainly heard people scream at the top of their lungs, "I am *not* angry!" And I suspect you have witnessed similar ludicrous attempts to deny emotions, problems, patterns, and strongholds.

2. *I admit to acting in a particular way, but it's not really a problem.* Megan has Irish ancestors, so after she snaps someone's head off she just shrugs and says, "It's in my blood."

   Daniel has had a string of one-night stands with women, but won't even consider making a commitment to any single one.

He denies having a problem, since it's "just a guy thing."

Carrie started with horoscopes, but has been getting deeper and deeper into things of the occult. She says, "It's important for Christians to know what other people believe."

By the time Megan, Daniel, and Carrie figure out they actually do have problems, they are likely to be unable to do much about them.

3. *You call it a problem. I say it helps me.* Gil, a power-monger, insists on his own way and sticks it to people who oppose him (when he can get away with it). But he says, "I do it for the good of my company."

Mark is unable to praise anyone because of his own insecurities. His defense: "I never got any praise, and I turned out OK." (That's what *he* thinks.)

Rose is always arguing with people. No one likes to deal with her, and she knows it. But she claims, "I think it's my spiritual gift to be the grain of sand everyone must overcome in order to form pearls." (I'm not making this up!)

All these people have strongholds that need attention. But until Gil, Mark, and Rose decide to be honest and admit that their quirks are actually problems, they will never grow.

Denial never works. The Christian principle of denying oneself has nothing to do with denying one's problems. There's nothing wrong with denying myself in order to put God first in my life. But denying my problems is not at all Christlike.

The antidote to denial is truth. When I begin to see myself as I really am and deal with that truth, then I can make good choices that will help me continue my search for freedom.

A problem similar to denial is **deflection.** Some people don't try to hide their problems, but it never seems to be their fault. When they see something unpleasant and unwanted in their lives, they respond one of two ways:

1. *It's because of a person or set of circumstances in my past.* Problems such as withdrawal, rage, or shame are frequently traced back to childhood. It's true that the problem may have originated then, but this is now. We need to consider present options and our personal responsibility. Many people blame parents or others who are now dead and gone. They assume, "I can't do anything about it now." But if you follow this logic, you conclude that such people can *never* be free. That is simply not the case.

2. *It's because of a person or set of circumstances I'm dealing with now.* You probably know people who always find someone or something to blame their problems on:

   - "I just can't deal with that person. She always brings out the worst in me."
   - "I would like to be more outgoing, but my husband would get jealous."
   - "People in my church would think I was terrible if I said what I really thought."

   People can always find an excuse for their problems. But they will never find *solutions* to those problems until they stop blaming others and take personal responsibility.

Remember, the *truth* sets us free. Denial and deflection both keep truth hidden—and we like it that way. But then we wonder why we never feel free, and we complain that life is so unfair.

Denial and deflection often surface in the lives of those who are overwhelmed by a fear of failure. Anytime they get close to dealing with a failure issue, they spend tremendous energy in denial. They feel that admitting the problem would be more painful than whatever pain it is currently causing.

Another reason we cling to denial and deflection is that our strongholds create a sense of structure in our lives. We don't want to give them up. At the same time, we crave freedom. But freedom without structure seems too frightening.

Would you be willing to hand out copies of a strongholds checklist to all the people who know you best and let *them* fill out which ones they think you have? If not, you may still be trying to keep from dealing with truth.

So I return to my original question: Do you think you are ready to demolish your strongholds, move forward with your life, and get involved in all the risks and rewards of freedom? If not, you need to identify what is holding you back and deal with it before you continue. And if you do feel that you are ready to move ahead, I have one additional question for you: Would you be willing to hand out copies of a strongholds checklist to all the people who know you best and let *them* fill out which ones they think you have? If not, you may still be trying to keep from dealing with truth. The root of bitterness may be embedded deeper than you think. So give this matter some thought before continuing ahead.

SAVING THE BEST FOR LAST?

Perhaps you are wondering why I waited until chapter eight to present the process of finding freedom. It is because I don't believe you can fully understand the answer until you better understand the problem. It's the same reason your math teacher wanted to see your work in addition to your answer. The answer itself doesn't mean a lot if you don't understand the process.

I suspect that God is reluctant to free us from bondage until we discover what put us there in the first place. He loves us too much. Otherwise, we would foolishly keep returning to the destructive habits that enslave us. We wouldn't know any better. But after our problems become strongholds, and after we finally see how they are formed and the damage they do, we aren't ever likely to grant them that much power in our lives again—not after experiencing freedom from them.

In the past you may have accused God of being powerless, uncaring, or distant. In reality, he is always patient and loving. He knows the extent of your pain, and he wants to provide an effective and permanent solution. In the meantime, however, most of us refuse to wait for a lasting answer. Instead, we do anything we can to handle the problem ourselves. But our strongholds cannot be demolished until we learn how they come into our lives, how we get used to them, how we allow them to have control over us, and how to resolve the problem God's way instead of ours.

So give the matter some serious thought. If you're really ready to remove those final obstacles to your complete freedom, let's move on. The next chapter focuses on God's part in the process.

Exercises for Chapter 8

1. Look back at the list of your personal strongholds that you identified on page 115. Think of how each of these individual problems grows out of the root of bitterness. Ask God to show

you which ones have the deepest roots. If you had to "dig up" the bitter root underneath the stronghold, which ones would be hardest to remove?

2. In your own life, can you list five (or more) different ways that bitterness has recently prevented forgiveness?

3. Have you ever forgiven without dealing with the bitterness that created the unforgiveness? What were the results of your efforts?

4. In what ways have you used each of the following techniques of denial to defend, rather than destroy, your strongholds?

   • "Problem? What problem?"

   • "I admit to acting in a particular way, but it's not really a problem."

   • "You call it a problem. I say it helps me."

5. In what ways have you used each of the following techniques of deflection to defend, rather than destroy, your strongholds?

    • "It's because of a person or set of circumstances in my past."

    • "It's because of a person or set of circumstances I'm dealing with now."

6. Can you think of any additional ways you defend your strongholds rather than trying to get rid of them? Be very honest with yourself as you consider this.

CHAPTER 9

Hearing God's Voice

T here is a structure to the strongholds that plague our lives. We were not aware when they were being created nor do we really know how they relate to each other. No tests, psychological or otherwise, will give us a diagram of how this internal structure has been created. Only God knows what it is like and how to dismantle it. Many have tried to look at Scripture or our faith as some simple cookbook. "Do the following, and you'll be OK." The fact is, truly experiencing what God has for us cannot occur without his moment-by-moment input. That's why I now turn to the vital issue of our hearing from God and his leading us into destroying these strongholds. No matter how well we might understand this book intellectually, we will not be able to directly apply these truths without first receiving our individual instructions from God.

Yes, personal, specific instructions directly from God to you. Does that idea make you feel a bit wary? Many people have struggled with this throughout history. In one of the darkest eras of all time, church leaders determined that they ought to keep "ordinary people" from being able to study the Bible for themselves. They did this by translating it in a language that only educated and "properly trained" clergy could understand. Those qualified scholars could then teach the rest of the people.

How could they justify taking God's Word away from God's people? They feared that if the Bible was made available for just anyone to read or teach, the laypeople would come up with different interpretations. And they were right. Some people's perspectives have led to divisions in the church, and others have tried to manipulate the teaching of Scripture to justify all kinds of foolishness.

Thankfully, a few brave souls saw that the potential benefits would more than compensate for the possible problems. They spoke against the official position of the church and prevailed. These days we distribute Bibles far and wide because we've seen the power of what God's Word can do—even in the hands of untrained and uneducated people.

Today another conflict divides the Christian community. At issue is the ability of "ordinary people" to hear from God. What seems to be the prevailing opinion—which may not be openly stated—is that the only people who "hear" God are frauds or those of suspect theological positions. Some well-known Christian psychiatrists even assert that if you say you hear from God, it's time for a little medication.

HOW SHALL THEY HEAR?

Many sincere believers have concluded that we are to receive every message from God through the words of Scripture alone. Certainly, no one is questioning the Bible is the Word of God.

However, Scripture gives many accounts of God speaking personally to people.

Some people would never expect God to reveal something from their past to help them demolish strongholds. They rule out the possibility of God communicating to individuals in personal ways. But I've seen it happen.

I was trying to counsel Peggy, but I was stuck. Peggy, in her late thirties, had had a difficult life. The dullness in her eyes was just one of the many signs of great sadness she carried like a heavy weight. All her life she had felt like an inconvenience to other people. She had been of no value to anyone else, so she thought, and felt she was even less value to herself. She had read and understood much of the Bible, yet it had not broken through her sadness.

We were about to close the session when God let me know it was time for an intervention from him. I told Peggy I felt we needed to ask God what he wanted us to know. I prayed: "Dear Father, please tell Peggy what you think of her." Then silence followed for about two minutes.

When I looked at her again, her eyes had a sparkle that had not been there before. With amazement, she said, "He told me that I was a precious flower to him. He said that he was taking the weeds away from me so I can live and grow."

Where could this thought have come from? Some might say it was simply a psychological wish being expressed. But if they worked with people struggling with deep depression, they would know this was not possible. I had not suggested what God might say to Peggy. In fact, we had spent our time that day exploring specific sad events in her life. Other people might suggest that this message came from Satan in an attempt to mislead her. Yet this is the last thing Satan would ever want this poor woman to hear. No, I believe this message came from God, just as I've seen God break through in numerous ways in other people's lives.

A FEW CAUTIONS

Yes, God does speak directly to us today. But let me give a word of caution. We have the ability to distort anything that comes from God, and hearing from God can be a prime example of this. So before we go any further, keep in mind the following.

Human beings can be deceived. Indeed, Scripture repeatedly warns us to be careful not to be deceived. Many people and forces claim to speak for God but do not speak the truth. Perhaps you recall reading about a "religious" group from Texas on their way to Louisiana. According to the spokesperson, God told them to remove all their clothes at the Louisiana border. They were pulled over somewhere along the way where the carload of naked people tried to explain to the skeptical officer that they were only doing what God had said to do. I suspect that this was not the first unusual thing they had done that they attributed, falsely, to God.

GUIDELINES FOR RECOGNIZING DECEPTION

First, *remember that God does not contradict himself.* He never has and he never will. He will not tell you to do anything that is inconsistent with what is recorded in his written Word. I've talked to numerous people who knew they were doing something contrary to biblical teaching, yet they firmly insisted they believed the Bible. They simply justified whatever they were doing by concluding that God had made an exception in their case. But God makes no exceptions.

Second, *seek input from someone who regularly demonstrates godly wisdom.* Such a person has likely heard from God personally at some point in his or her life. Someone who displays the peace and power of God over a period of time isn't usually difficult to pick out of a crowd. Try to develop good relationships with those who can help you in your process of spiritual maturity and offer you good advice when you need it.

Finally, *be suspicious of anything you hear from God that makes you feel driven in any way.* God allows us to *choose* to follow him. He never forces us or places us in situations where we cannot exercise our will with freedom. If you begin to feel compelled to do things you don't choose to do, you need to reconsider the source of your feelings. It isn't likely to be a message from God.

It is true that people do crazy and even harmful things and falsely attribute their actions to God's instructions. But does that mean God doesn't really speak to his children? If we use that argument, we should tell people to stop reading their Bibles because too many people misinterpret or misapply what they read. We mustn't let a few misguided people prevent us from trying to hear what God has to say to us.

A TWO-WAY RELATIONSHIP

Why do I make such a point about hearing from God? I think too many people don't understand God's desire to be actively involved in our lives. Some imply that with the completion of the Bible, God's communication to us also became complete. If so, he hasn't had anything to say in thousands of years now. Others suggest that communication to God is one-way. We "pick up the phone" and talk to him through prayer, but we never actually hear his response. I'm convinced we must get past these misconceptions and learn to improve our communication—both ways—with God. (In the next chapter I'm going to talk about our talking to him.)

Far too many Christians settle for the thoughts generated by their own minds. They may have a lot of human wisdom and possibly considerable Bible knowledge as well. But when they try to face life's challenges, they seem to keep coming up short. When serious problems arise, they turn to other people for additional help, perhaps even professional counselors, which frequently adds more human wisdom but little else.

It's not that God doesn't use human beings in spite of their limitations. He can communicate through a donkey if he so desires (and has done so). But human beings have human limitations. Many times even "Christian counseling" becomes adherence to just another set of formulas.

If we are to really find freedom, God is going to have to be the One who leads us there. I have seen countless people who have come to an apparent standstill in their progress after being in counseling for years. Yet these same people, once they depended on God to provide them (and their counselors) with understanding, were able to make tremendous breakthroughs.

I believe God sometimes speaks to individuals, and does so in a clear and enlightening way. I want to close this chapter with the story of one woman I know very well. She, like many others who might be reading this, could not remember ever having heard from God. For a long time, all this woman knew was that "something horrible had happened" to her—"someone had tried to kill her and they had almost succeeded." What that something was, though, eluded her, for she had no memories of it.

During eighteen months of agonized searching and prayer, which included a period of hospitalization, she still had no answers. More therapy, more hospitalization, more time—another year—went by, and she still hadn't been able to break through what was destroying her life. Finally, she was admitted to a hospital that specialized in treating disassociative disorders of the ritually abused. Here is her story in her own words.

Marisa, it turned out, represented a part of me, and as I refer to her, I tell of myself. I took her to the leading doctors in America... and they could not fix her. She would not or could not tell what had happened to her. She had no memories of what happened to her. All I knew was that something horrible had happened to Marisa—someone had tried to kill her and they had almost succeeded. Her very life was now hanging by a thread.

I put her in a very good hospital and she received the best care money could buy. After all, she was a born-again Christian and had been for years. Certainly, I could pray and ask God to heal her. However, God seemed strangely quiet.

Now I'm frantic. For eighteen months I've searched and searched for the answers of what happened to Marisa. I'm falling apart, and she's already fallen apart. I pray and pray. I pour out my heart in agony night after night. "God, you say you are all-powerful. Do something, do something!"

Finally after eighteen months of hell on earth, the Lord sent a woman to me, a woman who knew him. For over a year, this woman (whom I had never met) had experienced visions of a dark-haired woman screaming and screaming, silent screams that no one could hear. When she walked into my home, she gasped as she saw me; I was that screaming woman.

She was a Christian therapist and a really beautiful woman. I told her what had been happening and she suggested that I come and visit her and leave my prison behind. My weight had dropped to 106 pounds by now, and she feared for my life. I concluded that this friend might be my only chance, so I ran, got the shoe box, took off the lid and unwrapped Marisa and all her limbs. I told her that I had to get her fixed. She said, "God will teach you how to fix her."

Well, in another year, I was pretty exhausted. I took Marisa [a doll which represented this woman] to see a world famous doctor in Dallas. After a few days with no sleep, Marisa was admitted to a hospital for Disassociative Disorders and treatment of the Ritually Abused. I went with her. I was so tired that I felt that I might as well go into the hospital. It would be like a rest for me. Little did I know that the last eighteen months of horror and harassment were just boot camp for the war that was about to be waged for my very life. For in the hospital, I was to learn some of the things that happened to Marisa.

Now I was mad. "God, you let people abuse Marisa. Where were you? And you're just now telling me about it?" Did all those things happen to Marisa—like they happened to the other patients? Child pornography, incest, ritualistic abuse, torture, mind control, sophisticated programming, electric shock treatment, ritualistic abortion?

Marisa wasn't getting better, nor was I. I hired another therapist; my rationale, "Two are better than one." Where was God? Where is he now? When did this horror begin? When did it end?

One day I'm looking at the map of Israel in my Bible dictionary. I am sitting with the head nurse who did know Mr. God. I looked at that map of ancient Israel and it had a line through it. Judah was bigger than Israel. I looked at her and said, "Ask God if this is me." I pointed to this map, and particularly to the smaller Israel.

She bowed her head and prayed. When she lifted her head, she had a tear streaming down her face. I said, "Well, is this me?" And she said… "Yes." I looked at the other nation, Judah, which was bigger and stronger than Israel. I started screaming, I just went to pieces. God, no, tell me it isn't true! Tell me I don't have this other person living in me, created by these people. The next twenty-four hours I fought not to give up my faith in God, in Jesus; his love was torn to shreds. I no longer wanted to live.

I felt that I had been deserted and let down by God Almighty. The reality of having another personality in me was the most scary, horrendous thing I had ever known. What had Marisa done, oh, God, my God, my Daddy? What in the world had she done?

I was in a hospital for seven and one-half months. I was released to Sara [a Christian therapist] and her friends in England... and unfortunately I was not much better. Sara and her assistant sat down with me in the old manor hall in England. We sat next to a fire. They said they had a group of people praying for me who knew nothing of my history. They would get together weekly and share if God had spoken to them concerning me. Then Sara with her dark brown, almost black, eyes leaned very close to me and said... "We need a miracle, and that's what we're praying for."

She said, "Have you heard from God?" I said no, but I thought many times maybe... I heard from him. But I think I could have been wrong. I just know he calls me Israel.

"Well," she said, "We will pray that you hear from God."

That night, I was pacing the courtyard, thinking about how to get back to America when suddenly, I heard this voice: "Israel... are you saved?..."

"Yes, Father" I said.

"Well, get up and act like it, and quit listening to those voices in your head; listen to me."

"Could this be God?" I asked Sara. "Does he really talk to people like that?" She looked at me intently and broke into a big smile and shook her head up and down. "Yes, that's him."

So every morning for the next seven and one-half months, I ran out into the forests and to an abandoned house to talk to Mr.

God. Sometimes, we had lunch, and sometimes he just broke in to my constant thinking and spoke to me. On the subject of what I had to do as a child growing up, being abused, tortured, and drugged by a cult, the Lord told me that he cried. When I asked him how could he use or accept anyone so horrible as me, he replied, "Israel, would you have me be crucified again?"

One of the most unusual things he did was to show me what happened to me as a little two-year-old being abused by my grandfather, who was obviously a pedophile and pornographer. When he showed me what the abuse was, Mr. God and I were walking down a lane in the North England hills. He said, "Israel, keep your eyes on the horizon, do not let your head fall." Only when I did exactly what he said did the years of disassociation... forgetting... melt away. There I saw the pain and anguish of a tiny two-year-old at the hands of her grandfather.

Was this at the root of my distrust and fear and anger at God? I mean, the Father seemed more like a grandfather to me.

Mr. God would also ask me how I felt about what he had shown me. I would tell him that I felt angry, furious, I hated myself because I was so helpless and drugged. He would say, speak louder. I would say, "I'm MAD. I HATE HIM AND I HATE MY GRANDFATHER. I HOPE HE'S IN HELL." This went on for a while, until the dam broke and over thirty years of tears came rushing down my cheeks. And by the evening, peace, indescribable peace came over me. He had performed surgery, working his way toward the heart of stone.

One day, I was praying and complaining and feeling sorry for myself. Therapy with Sara and her assistant was slow, and I hadn't had any more memories in a while. I felt that maybe this was it. The Lord had told them he was going to heal me, but I didn't feel as if I were going anywhere. I was at the pit of discouragement.

As I was praying, I saw myself in a long, black dress. I was helping all these brides get ready for a wedding. They were young and beautiful and dressed in white. In fact, I knew some of them. I saw them walk out to go to their wedding... to meet their bridegroom... whom I believed to be the Lord Jesus. I was sitting all alone with a little beaded black purse in my hand. I heard God's voice, "Yes, Mr. God. I have nothing to give you. I have only a broken life, no talent, no virtue, no nothing."

He said, "Look in your purse." I thought, well there's nothing in there; I've already looked, but I'll look anyway. I see this scenario unfold in my head. I looked inside and in the very bottom, hidden in the folds of the black purse is a huge diamond ring. When I turn it over it is inscribed

To Israel

Love Jesus

I said, "What is this big engagement ring doing in my purse?" He said, "I took the ashes of a broken life and made them into a diamond. Israel, I love you."

Then a gigantic dam broke inside of me and the tears of an abandoned child flooded down my face. Mr. God loves me. Not because of the song, or church, or some well-meaning Christian. His Word came to life... and suddenly, I knew... God who loved the world and gave his only begotten Son, loved me. Little nobody me. He loved me... and my Daddy in heaven had come back for his daughter.

God is healing Marisa, and he is healing me. All the King's horses and all the King's men did put me back together again. The Lord Jesus is the King; he is my King. "With man this is impossible, but with God all things are possible" (Mt 19:26).

Again, let me repeat the importance of this material you have just read. I have labored the point of your hearing from God greatly because unless you hear God's voice, the truths in this book will not affect your life as they should. God is as much of an option in this process as making sure the beautiful car you buy also has an engine in it. Your experience with the Father will be different from anyone else's experience. Do not try to copy anything you have read here. The Father will create his time with you to be special and just what you need.

Exercises for Chapter 9

You may want to pray a prayer such as this one:

Heavenly Father,
    I would like to hear from you. The Bible tells me of your desire to communicate with your children. Your Word tells me that your sheep know your voice and follow you. I want to know your voice personally and I want to follow you. Please speak to me through my thoughts and tell me what you want me to know about myself, good and bad. I will be quiet and listen for your voice. Help me to recognize it when you speak to me.

CHAPTER 10

Prayer Paves the Way

◄▬

If I wanted to mow my yard I could go to the garage, take out my mower, and start pushing it in circles around my lawn. But would that get the job done?

It depends. As long as the mower was working properly, my efforts would not be in vain. But what if it didn't have any gas in it? What if the spark plug wire was disconnected? What if I neglected to start it before I started mowing? Any of these problems could prevent me from doing what I had set out to do. Not only would I be working hard with no result, I would also look silly to observers. And when I finally realized what I was doing, I might *feel* foolish as well.

Many times well-meaning Christians start praying without giving it much thought. We go through the right motions, just like a guy "mowing his yard" with no gas in the mower. Prayer, though, is more than saying the right words. People can pray with intense devotion and determination, yet see no more change in their lives than I would see in my lawn if I tried to mow with the mower turned off.

Much has been said and written about prayer. Certainly I cannot tell you all you need to know in one chapter, yet I think it's important to consider the importance of prayer as it specifically pertains to strongholds. In this chapter I want to focus mainly on preparing ourselves through prayer to confront the personal strongholds in our lives.

WHY PREPARE WITH PRAYER?

Why must we prepare in prayer before acting against our strongholds? Because *prayer connects us with God.* In the last chapter we discussed the futility of trying to combat our strongholds using our own power. When we do, the stronghold not only gets stronger, but it soon erects other strongholds that only intensify our emotional pain.

Prayer is the means by which we accomplish God's business on earth. We can run around on our own and achieve little if anything. But *prayer tunes us in to God's purpose for us.* Even Jesus devoted himself to prayer while he was here on earth. He was committed to knowing and carrying out his Father's will for him, and he remained true to God's purpose. People recognized that he spoke with authority. They knew, at least the wise ones did, that what Jesus told them came from God. His prayer contact with God kept him focused on his mission rather than the problems and unpleasantness he faced. Even during the pain of his crucifixion and death, Jesus prayed to stay in touch with God the Father.

Because we are spiritual beings, we should view our problems as spiritual problems. Strongholds position themselves in the soul, but they affect the body as well. If we treat them as physical problems, we never make significant progress against them. They are spiritual problems that require a spiritual solution. And in order for God to provide the spiritual help needed, we must communicate with him through prayer.

Prayer is also the method by which *we allow God to examine us and help us see where we really stand.* Without prayer, we overestimate our own importance and ability to handle our problems. As we draw nearer to God, however, and see what true holiness and righteousness really are, we are no longer deceived into thinking we're capable of helping ourselves.

God promises to give us the desires of our hearts (see Psalm 37:4). But if you're like me, it's easy to lose sight of what you really desire. I may think I want a lot of things that wouldn't actually satisfy me if I had them. Through prayer God makes us sensitive to our true needs. He helps us differentiate between worthwhile desires and the things that deceive us. As Paul makes so clear in Romans:

The Spirit helps us in our weakness. We do not know what we ought to pray for, but the Spirit himself intercedes for us with groans that words cannot express. And he who searches our hearts knows the mind of the Spirit, because the Spirit intercedes for the saints in accordance with God's will.
Romans 8:26-27

I cannot imagine trying to demolish strongholds without first preparing with prayer, though I know some people do. Any number of programs and suggested techniques are available to try. But it is like trying to diet without mentally preparing yourself to lose weight. If you're not ready to get serious and do whatever it takes—no matter how hard it might be or how much discipline is required—failure is much more likely than success. The same is true in the spiritual realm. If we're not prepared to receive God's help, we won't make much progress in our search for freedom.

ISN'T PRAYER REDUNDANT?

People frequently ask: "Isn't God all-knowing? Doesn't he know when I have strongholds that need to be removed?" Of course! So why, then, is it so important to pray just to tell him something he already knows?

God doesn't need any help destroying our strongholds. *We* do. Yet in many cases, people with strongholds feel very much alone. That's part of the nature of strongholds. They are not things we like to admit to ourselves, much less talk about with others. Prayer reminds us that we are not alone. It alerts us to the fact that God is not only all-knowing but all-powerful as well. Through prayer we begin to communicate with the one single force that can bring down the mighty strongholds in our lives.

Remember the widespread false belief that affects so many people: *This is the way I am. I've been this way all my life. And there's noth - ing I can do about it.* Satan wins many battles without a fight simply because he convinces us to leave God out of the picture. But by merely articulating one's need to God, we remind ourselves of the Source of strength that is always available to combat personal fears and Satan's lies.

An often quoted passage of Scripture is Proverbs 3:5-6: "Trust in the Lord with all your heart and lean not on your own understanding; in all your ways acknowledge him, and he will make your paths straight." In plain and simple terms, I think this means to *be aware of God*. Our failure to "acknowledge" God "in all our ways" gets us in trouble and then keeps us there. Prayer is the key out of solitary confinement and back into awareness of the One who can really help us.

Our prayers also initiate God's action. Sure, he already knows what we need. But as *we* realize we have specific needs or questions,

God begins to provide wisdom and answers. As we have seen, many times we can find answers in his written Word. Other times he might direct us to another person who has accumulated a store of godly wisdom and experience. And sometimes God might respond directly to our heartfelt needs and desires. God doesn't want us to suffer. I believe he sometimes allows our pain to intensify until we are motivated to do something to reduce or eliminate it. It may be difficult to see how a loving God could allow us to feel so much pain. Yet as soon as we realize how severe our problems are and how intense our pain is, and that we are incapable of coming up with our own lasting solutions, God is available with both the power we need to demolish our strongholds and the love we need in their place.

Our failure to "acknowledge" God "in all our ways" gets us in trouble and then keeps us there. Prayer is the key out of solitary confinement and back into awareness of the One who can really help us.

THE ANTIDOTE FOR PASSIVITY

The concept of prayer may generate ideas of formal rituals. "Praying to God" just sounds stuffy, pious, and unappealing. If the word *prayer* creates similar thoughts for you, think in terms of talking with God. That's what prayer is supposed to be. If we've made it something else, we've gotten off track. You don't have to kneel. You don't have to close your eyes. You don't have to whisper. Some of the most genuine prayers I've ever heard have been accompanied by tears of agony, shouts of despair, and smiles of relief. Others I wasn't able to hear at all, but I know that God heard and responded because of the incredible change in the person that nothing else had been able to accomplish.

Passivity is the worst enemy of Christians. Many times we sit around and wait for God—or somebody—to do something about the problems in our lives. Prayer is the best antidote for passivity. We often think *Since nothing else works, I guess I can pray about it.* That's precisely the wrong attitude. As soon as God allows us to see more clearly how our lives are being controlled by strongholds and how our freedom has disappeared, we need to turn to him in prayer. It's an active step. It's an effective action. And it calls into play the unmatchable power of God.

I can't tell you how many Christians approach counselors for help with chronic problems, usually strongholds, expecting us to be the change agents. When I ask, "What has the Lord showed you in this area lately?" they look surprised. Some even say, "That's why I came to see you." We must learn to communicate to God more effectively as individuals. No one else can fight our spiritual battles and destroy our strongholds for us.

We shouldn't turn to God just during crisis situations either. Most of the time, the reason we experience crisis is because we haven't been in touch with God on a regular basis. Here's a passage you may be familiar with, but take a close look at it one more time:

Rejoice in the Lord always. I will say it again: Rejoice!
Let your gentleness be evident to all. The Lord is near.
Do not be anxious about anything, but in everything,
by prayer and petition, with thanksgiving, present your
requests to God. And the peace of God, which
transcends all understanding, will guard your hearts
and your minds in Christ Jesus.
Philippians 4:4-7

I want to call your attention to the tucked-away phrase "in everything." Prayer isn't just for "big" issues in life. Anything that causes worry or anxiety should immediately be shared with God. If we can remind ourselves to seek his help for all the little problems we face, we aren't likely to find ourselves facing so many big issues. We beat passivity and immobility by going to God early and often with our problems.

Be aware that simply because you pray as you *prepare* to face your strongholds, you're not finished praying. Too many of us have a "saying grace" mentality about praying. We may have been taught by example that prayer is something you're expected to do—an obligation—before you get on with life. Pray before a meal, get it over with, and then dig in. Pack as much activity into the day as you can, and then have God bless it all with a quick "Now I lay me down to sleep" prayer just before bed. Go to church and use the prayer times to daydream or nod off for a few seconds. These habits are all typical of the way children pray. Too often, they are typical of adult prayers as well.

To demolish strongholds we pray before, during, and after the process. Doesn't this make sense? Since we've said prayer is simply talking to God, we're asking a Friend for help to destroy something before it destroys us. We wouldn't take the help of a human friend and then walk away without saying "Thanks," asking "What do I do now?" or communicating in *some* way. Yet, regretably, that's exactly how we tend to relate to God.

Preparation through prayer helps us submit to God. James 4:7 tells us: "Submit yourselves... to God. Resist the devil, and he will flee from you." This is a two-part process. First we are to submit to God. Then we are to resist the devil and avoid the problems that would otherwise result. We tend to want to skip the first step and jump right to the second one. Yet it does little good to try to resist the devil without first submitting to God. That's how our strongholds gain such power over us.

As we submit to God, we begin to love what he loves and hate what he hates. We start to see our strongholds as he sees them—destructive and evil. While we might have found them unpleasant, along the way we've learned to live with them. Perhaps we're even comfortable with the structure they give our lives, even though we're far from being free. Prayer helps us see that we've been living a lie. We see that strongholds must no longer be tolerated. Instead, they must be demolished.

One of our counselors was talking with a man addicted to pornography. The man told him, "I don't see that what I do is so bad." Yet the reason he had come for help was that his wife had left him and had taken the kids because his habit was so out of control. The man obviously liked pornography. He just didn't like what it was doing to him. The counselor suggested the man pray and ask God to show him what evil really was. He did, and it didn't take long for him to begin to see his situation from God's perspective. After submitting to God, the man was then able to do something to rid himself of his evil addiction.

WHAT SHOULD WE PRAY FOR?

When people ask me how to pray about dealing with stronghoIds, I suggest they pray to *have a genuine desire to be right with God.* We must be able to ask him to show us exactly what is causing the problem. Perhaps we've been avoiding this for a long time, but we must see the problem clearly before we can eliminate it.

We also need to ask God to determine the pace and direction for our spiritual growth. Satan boldly imposes himself into our lives, but God doesn't work that way. While God certainly limits the power of our enemy and continues to provide us with good things, we must ultimately choose to get him involved in our spiritual battles. If we insist on doing things our way, God will let us. That's why we said in chapter seven that it is so important to "keep in step with the Spirit" (Gal 5:25). If we find ourselves out ahead of God, we make ourselves vulnerable to attack and spiritual defeat. If we lag behind, we never even see what God has in store for us. It's important for us to stay in step with God. We cannot expect to go our own ways, wherever that might lead, and expect God to follow us. Prayer helps us find the pace and the direction to stay in step with God.

Prayer confirms who God really is. We are reminded as we pray that our strongholds are not God. The one responsible for deceiving us into building strongholds is not God. Only God is God, and his power is much greater than any other power. We take a giant step toward freedom when we enlist the help of God and stand in awe of his might and power.

Our prayers need to include *personal confession*. We tend to blame others for the wrong that was done to us. Certainly, much of that blame is justified. Yet almost always we find ourselves with sinful attitudes toward others. When blame becomes hatred, bitterness, and unforgiveness, we have crossed the line that separates justifiable response from sin. We need to confess whatever it is that *we* have done wrong. (I'll say more on this in chapter eleven.)

Prayer should also include *praise—whether we feel like it or not*. Preferably, our praise will be heartfelt, but that's not always the case. When we become emotionally hurt, many times we "clam up" and remain silent before God. We hide our anger. We keep replaying the offenses in our minds and sorting through the reasons we are hurt. We close ourselves off in our thoughts.

Yet we must learn to express ourselves to God during such times. We not only need to pray, but we need to go beyond the way we feel and determine to praise God as well. Just because we are suffering doesn't mean his power or love has diminished in the least. Again, emotional pain renders us passive. But boldly praising God in spite of our circumstances is an active and healthy step. We are exhorted in Hebrews 13:15: "Through Jesus... let us continually offer to God a sacrifice of praise—the fruit of lips that confess his name." Sometimes praise must be a sacrifice rather than a thrill, yet it may be exactly what is needed in a particularly painful situation.

UNCOMMON SENSE

If you've recently been through a lot of emotional pain, you may be thinking, *None of what you're saying makes sense.* To tell you the truth, I'd have to agree with you. You're already hurting, and I've told you to ask God to show you the source of your pain even more clearly. You feel as bad as you've ever felt before in your life, and I'm asking you to praise God. Perhaps you've even been praying all along in your struggles, and I'm expecting you to "start from scratch," so to speak. You're right. It doesn't make sense. At least, not common sense. Yet I am convinced God makes uncommon sense. I hope you'll have the faith and courage to see that for yourself. You don't need to reason everything out in order to try it. That's where faith comes in—not faith in me or even in what I'm saying. Put your faith in God. Believe that he loves you and wants to help you. Then when you pray, you will see results.

John Wesley once wrote, "God will do nothing, but in answer to prayer." If we let that thought sink in, we would be much more willing to involve God with our struggles early and to keep in touch with him on a regular basis. I don't think Wesley was ignoring the concept of grace. Rather, I think God graciously provides us a way to tap into his endless resources, and that way is prayer. If your levels of peace, freedom, and healing were directly proportional to the amount of time you spent in prayer, what kind of shape would you be in?

As soon as we commit to prayer, however, another principle kicks in. Look closely at this passage, which is itself part of a prayer: "Now to him who is able to do immeasurably more than all we ask or imagine, according to his power that is at work within us, to him be glory in the church and in Christ Jesus throughout all generations, for ever and ever!" (Eph 3:20-21).

A child may sheepishly ask her grandfather for a nickel to stick in the bubble gum machine, but Grandpa may demonstrate his love by taking her out for a banana split instead. Prayer opens us up to many wonderful surprises God might have in store for us. I see this all the time—both in my own life and in the lives of people I work with.

In most cases, we don't turn to God at all. Consequently, we usually get considerably more input from ourselves and the devil than from our loving heavenly Father. For this reason, prayer is more important than we may ever realize.

We need to remember that prayer is a powerful influence on someone else—our spiritual enemy. The fact that we pray and take our problems to God immediately weakens the enemy's hold on us.

For this reason prayer should frequently be spoken aloud. Satan does not have the same power as God to read our thoughts. The only things he can be sure are in our minds are the thoughts he places there. He can discern, to some extent, what we are thinking by observing our behaviors. But I like to recommend audible, spoken prayer. Many people experience a greater level of strength, courage, and encouragement when they pray aloud. Spoken prayer invites God's attention, invigorates the person doing the praying, and warns the devil to back off. It becomes clear that we are submitting to God, so Satan has no choice but to flee.

Think about the power of spoken words. Many of us with strongholds can trace the problem back to an instance where we were devastated by the impact of someone else's words. Many hurting adults still hear the harsh words of their parents or other people ringing in their minds. Every time we hear those words repeated, we relive the traumatic experiences of the past.

But words also have the power to heal. By speaking truth to God in prayer, we chip away at the power those former harsh words have held us in. Praying is not the same as psyching yourself up or playing mind games. When we pray, we know our words can lead to healing because they are being heard by a Great Physician with the power to heal.

GETTING STARTED

One of the best prayers I can recommend is straight from Scripture. It has been quoted in other sections of this book, but I'll use it again here because this is a different context. I really like the prayer of David in Psalm 139:23-24: "Search me, O God, and know my heart; test me and know my anxious thoughts. See if there is any offensive way in me, and lead me in the way everlasting."

Don't just repeat the words. Use the prayer as an outline. For example, take the time to list your anxious thoughts. Share them with God, one by one. As you do, God may reveal new ones that you hadn't even identified. He may guide your thoughts back to the origins of your anxiety. Then you might do the same with "offensive ways." (I can usually list plenty of offensive ways on my own before I ever need to ask God to inspect me.) Confess everything you can think of. And again, perhaps God will then gently prod your memory and clarify your spiritual vision to help you recognize new things you should add to your list.

Through prayer God shows us the motives behind our behaviors. We lost sight of them years ago, and today we suffer in ignorance. Truth sets us free, and only God is capable of helping us discern truth from all the current deceptions in our lives.

I also like to recommend "Show Me" prayers. For example:

- Lord, show me what's in my heart.
- Show me my first instance of turning away from you.
- Show me *why* I did what I did the very first time. (For example, taking drugs due to peer pressure, or having premarital sex due to lack of love from parents.)
- Show me how my behaviors made me feel back then, and how I'm really feeling now as a result.
- Show me why I established a destructive pattern and kept doing it.
- Show me how I've distorted your truth.
- Show me how I've been deceived.

You may wonder, *Why do I have to take this expedition into my past? Why worry about things that happened so long ago?* Because your strongholds may be more numerous than you think. Our goal is not to demolish *some* of our strongholds. If that's all we do, we're only going to substitute others in their place. What we must do is commit to demolishing *all* strongholds in our lives. Only then can we be free. Only then can we be sure that new ones will not immediately crop up again. But the only way to demolish them all is to *expose* them all. That's why enlisting God's help through prayer is so essential.

This concept may become more clear if we think in terms of specific strongholds. Let's say we're trying to eliminate the stronghold of alcoholism. Do you think you can simply confess it to God and immediately find complete freedom? Not likely. Even though you may submit to God in complete sincerity, you won't be any closer to freedom unless you allow him access to your past. Why did you start drinking to begin with? Was it depression? Was it insecurity? Was it fear? Until you get back to the original stronghold, you won't have dealt with the actual problem. You need to go back to the beginning and let God give you a fresh start.

A fresh start. Can you see how we've come full circle from the problems introduced in chapter one? We've had to learn to come face-to-face with our evil and depraved state. We've seen how that fleshly, natural state allowed strongholds to form. We've seen that a battle is taking place over the control of our souls. Much of what we've seen has not been pretty.

A lot can go wrong with our lives—a whole lot. But God can and will give us a fresh start. He will help us demolish every stronghold and find sweet freedom at last. And prayer is the key to making the difference.

Exercises for Chapter 10

Rather than assigning written exercises for this chapter, I would prefer to have you spend the time in prayer instead. Here are just a few ideas to get you started.

1. Leaf through the Psalms for other beautiful prayer expressions to God. (Psalm 139:23-24 is a great one, but by no means the only one.) As you find passages you want to remember and use again, record them below.

   •

   •

   •

   •

   •

2. Select one of the "Show Me" prayers (page 173) and focus only on that issue for a lengthy period of time. When you feel you've exhausted that particular area, move on to another one.

3. Remember that prayer should be two-way communication. If you find you are doing all or most of the talking, discipline yourself to remain quiet enough to allow God's Spirit to communicate with you.

CHAPTER 11

The Path to Freedom

W hen the Rapha* organization does seminars, we frequently use a checklist of many different strongholds similar to the one at the end of chapter six. We ask participants to check all that apply to them.

One woman filled out the sheet and checked almost everything. She was about thirty-five years old and had grown up with an alcoholic father who had abused her both physically and sexually. She remembers as early as age three lying in bed and trying to figure out how to kill her father before he killed her. All her life, she had tried various methods to cope with the pain and fear that her father inflicted.

The assignment at this particular conference was for the participants, between sessions, to write out (1) a list of attitudes stemming from their strongholds that were based on anger, resentment, hatred, or bitterness; (2) thoughts and feelings in the person's life

---

*Editor's note: See Appendix 2 for more information about Rapha. Robert McGee is the founder and president of this organization.

that reflected helplessness or despair; and (3) personal fears. In response to this assignment, most people jot down the first few thoughts that come off the top of their heads, and later we try to help them dig deeper and be more honest. But this woman needed no such prodding. Here are the results of her assignment, used with her permission. Please read these lists slowly. Put yourself in the place of a person who responded this way, and imagine what your quality of life would be like. Finally, consider how many of these responses are also true of your own life.

ATTITUDES OF ANGER, RESENTMENT, HATRED, BITTERNESS

At my DAD for his weakness.

At my DAD for abusing me.

At my HUSBAND for avoiding problems.

At my HUSBAND for rarely complimenting or noticing me.

At my BOSS for not being a good leader.

At my PASTOR for his lack of sincerity and truthfulness in dealing with me.

At my SON for continuing to fail, especially in areas that have gotten him in trouble before.

At my DAD for not loving me the way I wanted him to.

At my MOM and DAD for not listening to me.

At my MOM for not paying a lot of attention to me.

At my HUSBAND for not noticing when I was hurting emotionally.

At my DOCTOR for not talking to me about personal or important matters.

At my MOM and DAD for their lack of communication—they never asked questions, made comments about anything I said or did, or showed any interest in me.

At my TEACHER for not understanding me or even trying to understand me.

At my IN-LAWS—it seems they are never happy with what I do.

At my BROTHER because he often criticizes what I do or say.

At my SISTER for saying things to make me feel guilty.

At my HUSBAND because he doesn't know how to express love and affection.

At my MOM and DAD because they rarely encouraged me to get involved with anything.

At my MOM and DAD because I never felt I could confide in them or go to them with my problems.

At my MOM and DAD because instead of providing for my emotional needs, they gave me material things. (Example: Christmas)

At my GRANDPARENTS because whenever anything was missing around the house the kids were always blamed.

At my BROTHER because he is money hungry.

At my AUNT because she doesn't spend time with the family like I think she should.

At my CHILDREN because they are very irresponsible around the house.

At my DAUGHTER because of her temper and the way she gets angry.

At MYSELF because I respond to problems and confrontations by withdrawing and getting depressed.

At my DAD because he was an alcoholic.

At my DAD because he hit my brother and sister.

At my DAD because he treated Mom badly.

At MYSELF because I let people control me.

THOUGHTS THAT LEAD TO FEELINGS OF HOPELESSNESS OR DESPAIR

That my husband will never change.

That my husband will never love and understand me the way I want him to.

That my parents never gave me the comfort, security, or acceptance I always wanted.

That I can't love my husband until he changes.

That I'll never stop being angry.

That no one will listen to me.

That people won't be honest with me.

That I will always be depressed.

That I'll never grow spiritually.

That I can't read and understand my Bible even though I want to.

That I'll always be shy.

That I'll always be afraid.

That fear will overwhelm me.

That no one cares for me.

That I'll never let anyone get very close to me.

That I'll never be able to communicate effectively.

That I can't accept God's love for me.

That I'll never fit in anywhere.

That I'll always feel defeated and like a failure.

That I'll always hate myself.

That I'll always be overweight.

That I'll continue to be deceived and believe Satan's lies rather than being able to recognize and reject them and accept God's truth.

That I can't forgive myself.

That I'm a failure.

That I'll always be fat and ugly.

That I'll never break free from fear, anxiety, intimidation, timidness, self-pity, unforgiveness, despair, hopelessness, and rage.

That I'll never fully grow up and feel comfortable being an adult.

That I'll never feel special.

That I'll never feel loved.

That I'll never understand God.

That I'll never be able to do all that I need to do to keep out of bondage.

That I'll never be able to feel worthy of God's love and acceptance of me.

That I'll never stop letting things overwhelm me.

That I'll never truly trust God to take care of me.

PERSONAL FEARS

Anything new

Being loved

Men

God punishing me

Failing God

Going crazy

Disappointing people

Not being nice enough

Confronting people

My own anger

Taking risks

Being abandoned

Being punished by others

Being a leader

Being criticized

Not being liked

That I will always be alone

The future

Ending up like my parents

The dark—especially nighttime

Calling people on the telephone

Standing up for myself

Accepting good things about myself

Trusting people

Being rejected by people

Not being perfect

God rejecting me

Dying

Committing suicide

Losing control

Hurting people

Angry people

Being assertive

Being alone the rest of my life

Being worthless and useless

Making decisions

Never changing and growing

Being hurt by other people

Not being competent

That what I have been thinking about myself is really the truth

God loving me

What will happen if I lose weight

Talking in front of people

Saying anything that shows how I really feel

Not measuring up to everyone's standards

That God will reject me because of the garbage in my life

When people start being honest about their feelings and objective as they evaluate their actions, lists like these are not out of the ordinary. Once someone determines to get to the bottom of the problem, the bottom usually turns out to be much deeper than previously suspected. If you've attempted similar exercises, you may have some idea of the extent of the power of your strongholds. If not, you may be in for a surprise.

But I'm not finished with the story of this woman and her lists. The seminar leader returned to his room between sessions and was stopped by her. He could tell by her countenance that something was very different about her. He said, "She looked more free."

Then she told him, "I did it! Through these lists, God showed me what I need to do. I didn't realize what had tormented me all my life. I don't want to deal with these things anymore. I know that I still have a lot of work to do, and that getting past these things will be a process. But this step of being completely honest with myself was the biggest thing hindering me from living my life the way I wanted to live it."

We all have a natural tendency to assume that our problems are unique and worse than those of most other people. Two people can have essentially the same background and almost equal levels of pain and fear. One person might never appear to be distressed, while the other might look panicky almost all the time. Yet perhaps the first person is actually being less honest than the second. You can't always determine which people are suffering most simply by looking. Indeed, the panicky person may be much closer to dealing with the problem and finding freedom.

When people look at you, what do you think they see? Are you completely open, vulnerable, and honest about your feelings and problems? Or are you afraid to admit the truth to yourself, much less others? You need to be willing to let down all your protective walls and vigorously seek the truth as you prepare to deal with your strongholds. Otherwise, you won't be successful. If you aren't truthful with yourself, you can beat your head against the walls of your strongholds, and all you'll get in return is a headache.

A SCRIPTURAL BASIS

In John 8:32, Jesus says, "You will know the truth, and the truth will set you free." Lots of people are quick to repeat this verse to serve any number of purposes, but you need to keep several things in mind to make sure you don't misinterpret it. To begin with, Jesus was speaking "to the Jews who had believed him" (v. 31). Is it possible to hear truth and not be free? Sure it is. Thousands of people teach Sunday school, preach, sing, and deal with God's truth in various ways on a regular basis. Yet how often do we hear of some scandal where another of God's servants is caught in some kind of severe and public sin? It's not enough to intellectually know truth. We must know the truth experientially as well.

Intellectual knowledge can become dangerous if it is not put into practice. What we learn ends up as empty phrases that are never applied. Gradually, we lose respect for the truth, followed soon by a loss of awe for God, the source of truth. Many people think their intellectual knowledge of Scripture makes them more spiritually mature than others. Yet such people are not always better off for all their so-called knowledge. They are simply more prideful.

God's Word can be profitable only as the Holy Spirit provides understanding. Scriptural principles that are learned and applied apart from direct interaction with God may be worthless and perhaps even destructive. But when we include God in the learning process, he helps us know and experience the truth. In spite of the failure of some people to get past a "head knowledge" of truth,

God makes it clear that freedom is possible if we only put what we know into practice.

The second reference is one I've already cited in several places. But it's an excellent reminder by the Apostle Paul that, although strongholds exist and hold power over people, they are problems that can be overcome—under the right circumstances. He writes:

Though we live in the world, we do not wage war as the world does. The weapons we fight with are not the weapons of the world. On the contrary, they have divine power to demolish strongholds. We demolish arguments and every pretension that sets itself up against the knowledge of God, and we take captive every thought to make it obedient to Christ.
2 Corinthians 10:3-5

Read this passage again, slowly. Let the words sink in. Paul packs a lot of promises in this short paragraph. Let's pull out some specific phrases and see what we can learn about the situation we find ourselves in.

We live in the world. We may be God's people, but we live in the world with others who aren't. We are expected to not physically separate ourselves into little groups of saints but to live among those who need to know the Source of hope and freedom whom we serve. Of course, sometimes our interactions and relationships with other people are going to backfire and cause us pain and emotional distress. This cannot be avoided. Sometimes other people take advantage of us as children when we cannot defend ourselves, which leads to various strongholds as adults. The answer is not to stop living or to retreat from the real world. We must hold out for a better answer.

We do not wage war as the world does. First, we must assume that *a war is going on.* I will leave the specific nature and content of this war to your own interpretation, because few issues tend to divide Christians more quickly than this one. But we are in some kind of war.

Second, *we are expected to take part*—to "wage war." I have repeatedly emphasized that the greatest enemy of the Christian is passivity. We have no right to claim that we don't want to fight. This is a spiritual battle. If we do nothing, we're going to have some casualties inflicted upon us in no time. I know many people who complain continually yet never get actively involved in the battle.

Third, *the world* (defined as those who are without benefit of spiritual insight into God's truth) *can still identify problem areas of life and will attempt to handle them as best they can.* But the ways of the world are not usually the ways of God. Occasionally the two might overlap. Sometimes they will be diametrically opposed. Other times, it might be hard to determine. For example, much has been accomplished through the efforts of civil disobedience. Consequently, Christians sometimes use that method to attempt to change society. I cannot judge the motives of anyone or determine whether they are fulfilling the leading of God. I would warn, however, about jumping on any particular worldly bandwagon simply because it seems to work. If asked to join the efforts of such people, I could not do so unless I felt the clear calling of God in the matter.

The weapons we fight with are not the weapons of the world. Just because we aren't to use worldly methods of combat doesn't mean that God leaves us defenseless. Not at all! He arms us with weapons not accessible to other people. The armor of Christians is detailed in Ephesians 6:10-18. Truth is a supportive belt. Righteousness is a protective breastplate. Faith is a shield. Salvation is a helmet. And added to these defensive pieces is the Word of God that works as a sword against the enemies we face. These things are not available to people who do not know God. In the next section we look at additional weapons to use in our battles against our strongholds.

On the contrary, [our weapons] have divine power to demolish strongholds. Contrasted against the ineffective weapons of this world, God's weapons wield his power. And because his power is infinitely stronger than the power of the flesh, only his weapons are capable of destroying strongholds. These strongholds are so named because they are stronger than the flesh. It takes a higher power to destroy them. The flesh is no match for the power of any spirit—God's or otherwise. Strongholds exist because of the influence of ungodly supernatural forces. They can only be destroyed by God's Spirit, who is not only infinitely powerful but also is motivated by love.

We demolish arguments and every pretension that sets itself up against the knowledge of God. At one time Satan led a personal rebellion, setting himself up against God and attempting to place his throne above God's throne (see Isaiah 14:12-15). He was, of course, defeated. Now all he can do is exert his influence whenever he can to deceive God's people. He still "sets himself up against the knowledge of God" (2 Cor 10:5). God is truth. Satan is a liar. As long as we believe Satan's deceptions, we will not experience the freedom God intends for our lives. We will live instead as slaves to the strongholds that are built upon false beliefs.

We take captive every thought [including false beliefs] to make it obedient to Christ. What false beliefs? In many ways, the negative messages we learned as children continue to control us. That's why it's so essential to "take captive every thought to make it obedient to Christ" (2 Cor 10:5). This is a key step. It is one of those specific truths that must be experienced—not simply absorbed intellectually. Spiritual maturity means consistently conforming one's own thought life to the thoughts of God.

I was recently talking to God about how I somewhat resented having to trust him with a certain area of my life. In response, he asked me: *Who else do you want to trust with your life?* He got right to the root of the problem. My mind was embracing thoughts that were contrary to his thoughts. Very quickly I understood that indeed he was much more trustworthy than anyone else, including myself. *Especially* myself. I confessed that my heart did not have the confidence in him that I wanted to have. As he continued to deal with me on this issue, I saw clearly that a stronghold of fear had established itself in my life and was warring against my desire to have the confidence in God that I needed. I immediately determined to demolish it, using the process that follows.

THE CROP PROCESS

I've used several agricultural analogies throughout this book: roots, dandelions, thistles. It's easier for me to think about the growth of intangible things in terms of something I can see and relate to. But now I'd like to move from the lawn to the darkroom and introduce you to a photographic term: *crop.*

People unfamiliar with photography sometimes look through magazines and wonder how the photographers captured such incredible shots. A gnarled tree framed perfectly in the picture. The dolphin leaping out of the tank at Sea World suspended right in the center of the shot. The heroine holding the child in her arms, the glow of the raging fire reflected in her eyes and the silhouettes of other firefighters perfectly symmetrical in the background. *Your* photographs never turn out like that. *Mine* don't, either. So what's the secret?

The secret is a technique called *cropping*. Photographers can take what looks like a normal, average photograph and trim it down to remove the parts they don't want in the picture. The gnarled tree in the original shot may have been one of many, the others were cropped. The dolphin may have been part of a panoramic shot with lots of fuzzy people in the background. But it's easy enough to do away with the fuzzy parts to draw full attention to the desired action. The heroic rescue scene might have looked like any other shot, but symmetry could be found by eliminating some of the extremes of the photograph and keeping only the portions that were essential.

So when it comes to opposing the strongholds in your life, I can think of no better acronym for you to remember than C-R-O-P. Each of the letters of CROP represents a step in the four-stage process of eliminating the undesirable things in your life: *Confession, Repentance, Obedience,* and *Praise.* If bitterness is "part of the picture," you can CROP it out. And any other strongholds can also be demolished in order to help you focus more clearly on the positive aspects you want to emphasize.

Confession. We've tried to destroy our strongholds our own way and wind up saddled with bitterness and unforgiveness. *Confess* literally means "to agree with God." We need to agree with God that our strongholds are evil. We need to acknowledge our sinful behavior as a major obstacle on our road to freedom.

Most Christians don't understand confession. Those who com-

190 The Search for Freedom

prehend it only partially understand it. I know this has been my case. I believed that confession entailed agreeing with God as to the reality of sin in my life. But that was the extent of it.

Suppose I told a lie. I could then agree with God that I had indeed lied, ask him to forgive me, and I would feel that I had completed the act of confession. But with this system of easy confession, I would find it pretty easy to lie again.

True confession of sin is more than agreeing with God about the *actuality* of sin. It must go beyond and help us to realize the reality of sin's destructiveness. Until we see evil for what it is, we will never understand the full depth of God's forgiveness.

Connie had been used and abused. She felt her hatred of certain other people was both justified and reasonable. But her hatred spread quickly until it was no longer isolated to those who had hurt her. The least offense against her, even by those who wanted to help, would immediately bring down her wrath on them. People learned to keep their distance, and Connie concluded that God was ultimately responsible for all the pains that she had experienced.

One day she was in a group where she was encouraged to speak about her feelings toward God. Out of her mouth came a litany of foul language that shocked her. For the first time she realized how holding on to the hatred of others had poisoned her very soul. Once she saw the true nature of her sin, she wanted to be released from it.

When I first learned to confess my sin, I sat under a tree with a sheet of paper and made a long list. I soon discovered that this was much too quick—that there was considerably more involved. The steps that follow in the CROP process will not lead to freedom unless confession is complete. I don't mean that you must recall every single wrong thing you've ever done before you can move on. Rather, as God reveals an area of sin to you, do not move on to the next step until you have seen how destructive this sin has been.

In addition to helping us see the destructiveness of our sin, confession helps us by revealing the connectiveness of our sins. I may be confessing, for example, the sin of lying. God may show me how my lying is connected to pride or a need to keep everyone pleased with me. Or the lying may be a "screen" to keep some other area of life from exposure. Our sins are usually connected to other sins. If we allow God to show us the connections, we can clear out a network of evil from our lives.

With confession we are dependent on the Holy Spirit to show us: (1) our surface sins, (2) how each sin might be connected to other sins, and (3) the extent of destructive evil in our lives due to our sins. Attempting to discern these things apart from the Holy Spirit will only lead into morbid introspection and the unveiling of hurts that will not be comforted.

Many counselors, however, believe that anything you can uncover must need uncovering. Without the guidance of the Holy Spirit, a counselor can lead a person through tremendous torment. We don't need to uncover everything in confession—just what God reveals. He knows exactly how much we are capable of handling.

Repentance. Our relationship with God is equally important in the second step of the CROP process—repentance. The concept of repentance is one of "turning back." Through repentance we turn from our self-willed approach to life and reestablish a face-to-face relationship with Jesus.

We often think repentance involves promising to do something to become more worthwhile to God. By focusing on our performance, however, we miss out on what it really means to be in a relationship. When we truly relate to God, we can do no less than relate to him as Lord. We must accept his leadership in our lives through the Holy Spirit.

Some people find it hard to accept such a complete yielding to

God, especially those who have lived with great hurt in their lives. For many of us, the priority list of life goes something like this:

1. Air

2. Water

3. Food

4. Control

Ironically, the more we need to control, the less control we have. Fear begins to rule because we feel that if we lose control something bad will happen to us, something hurtful, so we refuse to yield to anyone—including God. As a result, we're saddled with all the fears and hurts that go along with such a great responsibility.

We who have lost the ability to trust others find repentance a difficult step. Trust is a precious commodity. But the challenge held out to us is this, "Taste and see that the Lord is good; blessed is the man who takes refuge in him" (Ps 34:8). Through repentance we "turn back" the control of our lives to God. He's the only one capable of handling it without all the hurts and fears that would otherwise result.

Associated with repentance is reliance. All our lives we have relied on the patterns of our childhood. We cannot be in a state where we are not reliant on something or someone. We will rely either on the patterns of our flesh, or the guidance of the Spirit. Scripture states this clearly in Galatians 5:16 when it says, "Walk by the Spirit and you will not carry out the desires of the flesh" (NAS). Unfortunately, we often try to turn from something without turning to the God who can set us free. Pray for the courage and faith that only God can give so that you can repent and rely on God.

Obedience. Our confession and repentance must come out of a viable relationship with God. The same is true about the third step of obedience. But in this case, we need to turn our attention to God's power.

By the time we discover strongholds in our lives, we also see that we are incapable of doing away with them using our own power. If we are to discover what God can do through us, we must learn to respond to him differently than we have in the past. If we have failed to respond to him, or have responded in wrong ways, we need to change how we relate to him.

Many of us have no confidence in our ability to respond differently. We groan at the thought. In addition, some of us have strong negative perceptions of obedience. We think obedience means having to do something against our wills or facing the consequences. But if our confession and repentance are genuine, we should see things from God's perspective. Obedience shouldn't seem like such an unpleasant alternative. It's a change of response that we should be more than willing to undertake.

If we have prepared through true confession and repentance, we have tapped into God's power to confront the darkness of our souls. Now it's only natural to want to keep the relationship strong as we seek to overcome the darkness and evil.

Does this mean our battle against evil is won—over and done with? Not by a long shot. That's why obedience is such an important step. Continued obedience results in continued victory. But it's easy to revert to our old, self-centered ways. When we seek to take back the control of our lives, we set ourselves up for failure. Yet God is quick to forgive us when we see the error of our ways and turn back to him.

Recall the incident of Peter's walking on the water to meet Jesus (see Matthew 14:22-33). Peter was able to show faith in Jesus to the extent that he walked across the water to meet him. What an amazing example of trust and obedience! But what happened? Peter took his focus off Jesus and transferred it to the circumstances around him—the wind, the waves, and the fact that he was standing on top of the water.

Yet if I'm going to make mistakes in life, I want them to be like Peter's. It is said, "To fail, you must first try." Jesus gently chided Peter for "little faith," yet it was clear that the reason Peter failed was because he had tried something others were unwilling to do. When the disciples got back to shore, at least Peter had gotten his feet wet.

When it comes to obedience, we can learn by trying even if we fail. *Notice that Peter was not punished for his failure.* Jesus reached out and lifted him up. A far worse mistake is to refuse to change how we respond to God and fall back into the same patterns that have always controlled us.

Confession. Repentance. Obedience. These things are difficult to get started. They require a new and different way of relating to God. Yet once we start, they begin a cycle of freedom that replaces the cycle of bondage caused by our previous patterns.

Praise. We are commanded throughout Scripture to offer praise and give thanks to God. Sometimes praise comes naturally. When things go our way, we rejoice and are thankful. But how about those times when we're feeling pain or depression? During those times praise is definitely not natural.

I believe praise is the highest form of spiritual warfare. David wrote: "You are enthroned as the Holy One; You are the praise of Israel" (Ps 22:3). After genuine confession, repentance, and obedience, praise is not optional—it's automatic. The first three steps will produce freedom from our strongholds and an overriding sense of freedom in our lives. As we experience this freedom that only God can provide, our hearts will praise him.

The CROP process, from start to finish, seeks change in our lives by changing and correcting our relationship with God. Consequently, the results are real and lasting. We can do no less than praise him.

GOING THROUGH THE *CROP* PROCESS

It may be difficult to theorize how the four-step CROP process works, so let's walk through the process with a specific example. Since bitterness may be the root of the other strongholds, let's see how we might go about getting rid of it.

Confessing Bitterness. Many of us are blinded to how many of the significant events in our lives can be traced back to bitterness. So we need to pray that God will search our hearts and find anything that might be there. As we yield to the illumination of the Holy Spirit, we might recall events we have not thought of in years. Again, it's not important for us to "rack our brains" in attempting to remember everything. Allow the Holy Spirit to bring the truth to light.

It's also important not to argue with the Spirit when such things are revealed. Our first instinct will be to defend our actions. Often, due to hatred and self-pity, we give ourselves permission to react in destructive ways—rebellion, drug use, sexual activity, withdrawal, self-will, or passivity. All these things are connected to bitterness, and we need to deal with each stronghold.

Ask the Holy Spirit to show you how these responses have destroyed or limited your life. Take your time. Unless you experience with God what these improper responses have done to your life, you will not be ready to go forward. When God says you have seen enough and you have confessed these things, *then* you are ready to go to the next step.

Repenting of bitterness. Bitterness and its related behaviors are the products of a self-willed life. The thought of living any other way will be frightening. You may have heard about, talked about, and sung about the lordship of Christ for most of your life. But at this stage, when you actually begin to experience it, you may experience a sensation of death within your soul. You are, in fact, putting to death your old ways of responding to life. This will feel uncomfortable and frightening at first.

Yet you'll quickly discover that the fear of the Lord is by no means as discomforting as the other fears you've had—fears of inadequacy, of the unknown, and of never being able to eliminate the pain you're feeling. As we repent and turn back toward God, there will be an awesomeness about the experience. We clearly see who we are only by first seeing clearly who he is.

Obedience as a replacement for bitterness. Much of our behavior is not what it should be due to the bitterness we have harbored for so long. Consequently, this might be a lengthy and difficult step. God has shown us the problem areas and we have repented of them by agreeing that they are wrong and seeing the extent of their destructive influence. But now we have to replace each of those errant behaviors with obedience to God.

In some cases, we already know what we're supposed to do. In other instances, however, we might need to continue to search God's Word and seek his will for how to stop being so bitter. Again, take your time. God does not reveal problems without also revealing solutions. As we begin to conform to his will in the ways we know how, we will begin to see what we need to do in the other areas as well. It is through obedience that you see God's complete power over the stronghold of bitterness, as well as the work he has already accomplished in your life.

Praise for victory over bitterness. The struggle against bitterness has been a long and difficult one, even with God's help. It has taken time and energy to see the extent of the effects of bitterness in your life. It has been painful to repent of each of these things. Replacing improper behaviors with godly ones has taken a lot of effort as well. But it has all been worth it.

When you experience release from the devastating weight of bitterness, joy will fill your soul. Lightness will accompany your step. Praise will flow from your lips. The newfound feeling of freedom will affect everything you do.

You don't have to understand it. You *can't* understand it. Just enjoy it and appreciate it. "Do not be anxious about anything, but in everything, by prayer and petition, with thanksgiving, present your requests to God. And the peace of God, which transcends all understanding, will guard your hearts and your minds in Christ Jesus" (Phil 4:6-7).

PUTTING IT ALL TOGETHER

Going through the CROP process will probably be difficult at first. You'll be dealing with things you haven't done anything about for years. But as you begin to use the steps of Confession, Repentance, Obedience, and Praise on a regular basis, the process won't seem nearly as cumbersome.

Since you're following the same pattern, you'll quickly become accustomed to going through the steps. What follows are some sample prayers that reflect the CROP process. While these samples are abbreviated, you can see that after your initial struggles to see your strongholds fall, the CROP steps can be short and effective. I have filled the blanks with sample answers. You can substitute your own to fit your circumstances.

Lord Jesus, I have *(hated)* my *(mom)* because she *(shouted at me)*. I agree with you that this is sin. Thank you for forgiving me. I now destroy this stronghold of *(hate)* in the name of the Lord Jesus Christ. I now choose, by my own free will, to forgive *(my mom)* for *(shouting at me)*. From now on, when I remember *(my mom shouting at me)*, I will choose to remember *(her)* as forgiven. Thank you for the truth that is setting me free.

* * *

Lord Jesus, I have *(been self-righteous and I think I am superior to others)*. I agree with you that this is sin. Thank you for forgiving me. I now destroy this stronghold of *(self-righteousness)* in the name of the Lord Jesus Christ. Thank you for the truth that sets me free.

* * *

Lord Jesus, I have *(been rebellious against my dad)*. I agree with you that this is sin. Thank you for providing the truth that sets me free.

* * *

Lord Jesus, I choose, by my own free will, to forgive myself for *(adultery)* because you have forgiven me. Thank you that your truth is setting me free.

* * *

Lord Jesus, I acknowledge that I have *(participated in asking questions using a Ouija Board)*. This is sin. I renounce this act. Thank you for forgiving me. I now consider this stronghold destroyed in the name of Jesus.

* * *

Lord Jesus, I have allowed myself to feel *(hopeless in my marriage)*—this is sin. You have told me my hope is in you. Thank you for forgiving me. I now destroy the stronghold of *(hopelessness)*.

As you can see, the CROP steps follow a definite pattern. But the actual language and expression is up to you. Make it personal. Mean what you say. And don't stop until your strongholds have fallen.

WHERE ARE THE WEAPONS?

In the previous discussion of 2 Corinthians 10:3-5, I said I would tell you about "the weapons we fight with" which "are not the weapons of the world." By now you may be wondering: *What are these special weapons that have "divine power," and where can I acquire an arsenal of my own?*

The only weapons you need are the ones just described in this chapter: confession, repentance, obedience, and praise. These are more than nice habits practiced by good people. When handled correctly, they are weapons. No stronghold—not even Satan himself—can stand against them. If you make the CROP process a regular practice in your life, you should see your strongholds begin to fall.

Can you again be victimized by your strongholds? From now on, that will be up to you. Strongholds can only be formed when you let a problem go unattended for a long period of time. When you were younger, you didn't know any better. Your strongholds took advantage of your childhood patterns, your fears, and your desire to avoid pain at any price. Now that you can see things a bit more clearly, you can eliminate those strongholds. They will try to come back. However, you will have destroyed the power of Satan in those stronghold areas.

This time you should notice when the strongholds begin to form again. You already know the terrible amounts of pain they will cause if you don't do something. And you have an effective four-step process (CROP) to do away with them. So as long as you continue to draw on God's power to face down your strongholds, they should never regain control.

And do you know what? You're going to experience the freedom God has been wanting you to have all along! You will finally be able to know what Jesus meant when he said we could have "life, and have it to the full" (Jn 10:10). By leaving your bondage behind, you will be entering a fresh new life. Your long search for freedom is finally going to see some results.

Exercises for Chapter 11

1. Go back through the woman's lists on page 178. Place a check beside anything she wrote that would also be true for you.

2. In the space below, add your own responses in each of the three areas:

   Attitudes of anger, resentment, or bitterness:

   Thoughts that lead to feelings of hopelessness or despair:

Personal fears:

3. Choose just one of the things you've listed (or checked) and spend the following week going through the CROP process. Focus on that single area unless God directs your thoughts to other related strongholds that are interconnected.

CHAPTER 12

Avoiding Common Failures
and Setbacks

T hink back to the last time you were hopelessly lost—a time when you had no idea where you were and couldn't get your bearings. Do you remember how you got into that situation? There are times, surely, when you've been in a new environment with no map and no sense of direction. You didn't know your way around.

Other times, though, you are looking for someplace you've been before, with a map and clear directions in your hand, and signs clearly posted—yet you just can't seem to find the place. Sometimes our minds are on something else, and we end up taking an unexpected detour.

I bring this up because I don't want to mislead anyone or oversimplify what I've been saying. The CROP principles are a "map to freedom," but be warned! Not everyone finds their way out from under their strongholds. I believe the principles of confession, repentance, obedience, and praise are powerful enough to free any-one. I believe these four steps will work in almost any set of circum-stances against any stronghold. But just as we sometimes take wrong turns in spite of all the maps in our possession and signs posted along the way, we still sometimes miss out on the freedom that CROP can make possible. Below are some of the most com-mon reasons why some people "just can't seem to break free."

"I'VE TRIED THIS BEFORE, AND IT DIDN'T WORK FOR ME."

There's nothing new about confessing sins, repenting of wrong-doing, obeying God, or praising him. So when the CROP progres-sion is presented to some people, they don't give it a chance. They may not say it, but they think, *Yeah, I've tried "religion," and it didn't work. I'm sure it helps some people, but not me.*

Other people say, "I know someone who tried something like this, and he's more messed up than ever." These doubts are what Scripture calls "fiery darts" or "flaming arrows" (Eph 6:16, NAS). We are given the pieces of armor discussed in the previous chapter (see Ephesians 6:10-18) as well as the "weapons" of confession, repentance, obedience, and praise to ward off these very attacks.

I took a chemistry course as a freshman in college where you were supposed to conduct a series of lab experiments to identify the mysterious substance in the test tube. On numerous occasions I wanted to tell the professor the book was wrong because I wasn't coming out with the right conclusions. But instead I learned to go back through the steps and see where *I* was in error. You and I need to do the same when the CROP process seems ineffective.

Any bad experience from the past can be dredged up as an excuse for not seeking freedom today. That's actually part of the stronghold's control over a person. Chances are good that people have never squarely faced the truth—and the pain—of their stronghold and then set out to destroy it with God's help. Such people simply won't give the process a fair shot.

I've spoken to many who say they have "sort of" done what God wants them to do. They seem to think God ought to be impressed that they "sort of" did what he said, and they expect him to do the rest for them. The process just doesn't work that way.

"MY CASE IS WORSE THAN OTHER PEOPLE'S. GOD CAN'T FIX ME."

By the way some people respond, you'd think they had a huge trophy reading "World's Greatest Stronghold." By definition, strongholds are awful, powerful, terrible, and disgusting. Everyone with a stronghold has done some embarrassing and humiliating things in the past. We cope however we can against these massive problems, and many of the things we try aren't effective. But that's no reason not to try other new things that will work.

This excuse places limits on God's power. The first sin committed on earth took place when Adam and Eve were deceived into thinking that God couldn't or wouldn't do what he said he would. The same lie works just as well today. Countless thousands of people remain in bondage because they don't think God is strong enough or willing enough to set them free.

"I'M AFRAID. WHAT HAPPENS IF I TRY AND FAIL?"

The fear of failure has been mentioned several times throughout this book in connection with strongholds. But nowhere is it more tragic than at this stage. Sometimes people see their problems with clarity. They know exactly what they need to do to get rid of them. The strongholds are causing them incredible pain and suffering. Yet the people continue to do nothing because they fear the solution won't work! What do they have to lose?

It's as if they have lost most of their hope of getting well. They aren't willing to risk the little that remains. As long as they do nothing, they can always hope that their problems will dissipate by themselves. They think that if they try something else and fail, they risk losing that tiny bit of hope they have left.

But they don't really understand the problem of strongholds. Without overcoming their passivity by taking some kind of action in God's power, those problems are never going away. Indeed, they will only get stronger and harder to deal with.

Living by faith is a lot like operating a pump that must be primed before water will come out. The pump sits over a well, with a little jar of water beside it. A thirsty man who comes across the pump has one of two options. He can drink the water in the jar, which will alleviate some of his thirst for a short while. Or he can pour the water into the pump while working the handle, and an abundant supply of fresh cold water will come gushing back out (from which he can replenish the water in the jar for the next time he gets thirsty).

If we direct the little bit of faith we have toward God, he will provide us with "immeasurably more than all we ask or imagine" (Eph 3:20). But too many of us carry our tiny bits of faith around in jars, taking sips to try to keep from starving, and wondering how long it will be until we run out altogether.

"I DON'T WANT THE RESPONSIBILITY OF FREEDOM"

While some people are afraid of seeking freedom and not succeeding, others are reluctant to risk freedom because they fear they will succeed. They realize their strongholds are a prison, yet they've learned to cope with them. They now know their way around. The pain is intense, but they are managing it... so far, at least. They may even realize that it's a fairly sick way to operate, but hey, it's gotten them this far hasn't it?

It scares them to consider change. It may also be that they feel other people understand they have "problems." If they become free of their strongholds, what will happen? What does it mean to take responsibility for their own lives? What will happen the first time they are expected to respond to someone and actually think about what they want to say and how they want to behave? These aren't questions they're ready to deal with. Not now, and maybe not ever. The thought of freedom is just too scary.

"THIS FREEDOM STUFF IS JUST ANOTHER ROLE TO PLAY, RIGHT?"

Some people have been role-playing so long that they don't seem to know how to do anything else. Their relationships have been messed up so badly that they have lost sight of what real relationships are supposed to be. So when they consider making changes in how they relate to God, they think in terms of "acting out another script" rather than correcting a dysfunctional relationship.

People who substitute routines for relationships have a lot of trouble when it comes to freedom. The unstructured nature of freedom is too much a contrast from the comfortable roles—actually, ruts—they have become accustomed to. With strongholds in control, they can play their roles and get by. Without them, they become lost, uncertain what to do, and perhaps even panicky.

"I GAVE IT A SHOT, BUT FORGET IT. I QUIT!"

Some people simply quit too soon. And this is perhaps the most tragic of all the excuses. The people are hurting. They desire freedom. They don't enjoy being controlled by their strongholds. Yet the pain generated by trying to break free seems too much for them. Just when they get to a breakthrough point, they give up.

Quitting before acquiring freedom makes it very difficult for a person to attempt the CROP process again. Patience and perseverance are required to get all the way through. Whenever someone quits too soon, he or she rarely ever wants to try again. This excuse then recycles into the first one on our list: "I tried it, and it didn't work."

If we do overcome these inner obstacles, however, what can we realistically expect? You will begin to experience freedom from the compulsiveness of the responses related to the stronghold. That does not mean you will never be tempted to take that old route again. But as long as you stand firm against doing this, you will be free from the "drivenness" that the stronghold now creates.

Exercises for Chapter 12

1. Which of these reasons have you used before to excuse yourself for not getting rid of strongholds in your life? Give specific examples in each case.

   - "I've tried this before, and it didn't work for me."

   - "My case is worse than other people's—God can't fix me."

   - "I'm afraid—what happens if I try and fail?"

- "I don't want the responsibility of freedom."

- "This freedom stuff is just another role to play, right?"

- "I gave it a shot, but forget it—I quit!"

  Do you still feel a need to use excuses, or do you feel you've gotten beyond that point? Explain.

2. If you don't yet feel free:
   - Are you confused about any of the material that has been presented? Describe what it is, specifically, that you're unclear about. Then reread those sections of the book and discuss your questions with someone you can trust.
   - Is fear preventing your moving ahead? In what ways?

   - What do you think it would take before you became ready to try to demolish your strongholds for good? Be very specific.

3. If you do feel free:
   - What do you think will be your biggest hindrance to continued freedom from here on?

   - What temptation are you almost sure to encounter that you should prepare yourself for now?

- How has your perspective changed in regard to:

  Your problems/strongholds?

  Yourself?

  God?

  Life?

4. What has God shown you since working toward demolishing your strongholds?

CHAPTER 13

Where Do I Go from Here?

What you've done has been incredibly difficult. You have confronted issues you've been avoiding since childhood. You have dared to choose a new and different way of living. You've committed to whatever effort is necessary, even if it causes pain, to rid yourself of the destructive patterns that have established themselves in your life. And ultimately, you put enough faith in God for him to provide you with the power to break free of your strongholds. You saw them demolished before your eyes. Quite impressive.

In another sense, however, all you've done is dig up a root. You corrected some mistakes of the past. And while you have broken free, your new freedom doesn't come with an automatic lifetime warranty. You are free to return to your former way of life if you so choose. So even after all the work you've already done and the pain you've already experienced—don't get too comfortable.

The primary benefit of freedom is that you are now able to choose to become the person God created you to be. You may not be

Superman or Wonder Woman, but "if anyone is in Christ, he is a new creation; the old has gone, the new has come!" (2 Cor 5:17). You didn't have that choice when your strongholds were in control. But now you are capable of obeying God more completely than ever before. You have dug up the root of bitterness, but you need to plant what you want in its place, or the weeds will return.

This time is critical for you. It is a time when, for many people, the sin of pride will try to creep in: *I did it! I'm stronger than I thought. If I can demolish that tough old stronghold, I can do anything! Hooray for me!* But wise and grateful people will instead turn their praise toward God and ask him to fill their newly cleaned out souls with his Holy Spirit.

Now many of those Bible verses that never meant a lot will take on a fresh new meaning. Perhaps you never knew what it meant to pray, "Deliver us from evil." Now you do. All those obscure references to "submitting to God" should now make sense. If you submit to anyone or anything else, your strongholds will return with all their pain and power. When you submit to God, the devil must flee (see James 4:7) and you will remain free. Many other passages will also "leap out" at you as you learn to live with your newfound freedom.

SURPRISE! SURPRISE! SURPRISE!

This book has come out of my experience. These aren't philosophical concepts I'm trying to describe for you. I went through a lot of emotional pain stemming from the strongholds in my life, and I, too, struggled through the CROP process.

I can't say I'm "out of the woods" yet. I don't think we ever are. Many of the biblical heroes who accomplished some of the biggest successes for God committed major sins later in life, after they had "gotten comfortable"—Noah, David, Solomon, and Gideon to name a few. So our newfound freedom should be accompanied by a word of caution and a challenge to remain obedient.

As I reflected on the process I went through, I observed three major surprises about life. As I close this book, I would like to share them with you. Then you can add your own discoveries to the list.

Surprise 1: Evil is much more powerful and has a far greater impact than most of us realize. We tend to become too casual when we discuss "good versus evil." Our battle is never over. There can be no truce. It's a fight to the finish. Satan, who knows he is already defeated, has nothing else to lose. He "prowls around like a roaring lion looking for someone to devour" (1 Pt 5:8). Nor can God, who is the originator of "every good and perfect gift" (Jas 1:17), compromise with evil. His will be the ultimate victory. But in the meantime, we're in the middle of the battle, and we're in for an ongoing, frequently unpleasant struggle. We must learn to overcome. "And they overcome him because of the blood of the Lamb and because of the word of their testimony" (Rv 12:11a, NAS).

The nature of evil may be even worse as we get older, because we begin to defend it rather than eliminate it. People we know and consider "good"—perhaps even ourselves—can be consumed with more evil than anyone would ever suspect. We become victims of war. And the only way to stop being a victim is to pick up the weapons God provides—salvation, truth, righteousness, faith, his Word, confession, repentance, obedience, praise, and so forth—and join the fight.

We are incapable of eliminating the evil in the world. God will do that eventually. But in the meantime we can eliminate it *in our lives.* And we can help lessen the suffering of the people around us. Once we destroy the power of the strongholds, we see more clearly how to break the patterns that we're passing along to the next generation as well. And we can share "battle strategies" with friends and associates.

This is an evil world we live in—much more so than I ever realized before.

Surprise 2: God is greater than we can know or imagine. Just as my understanding of evil was severely limited, so was my understanding of God. I was a Christian. I had a good knowledge of Scripture. I *thought* I knew God. But after experiencing freedom from my strongholds, I quickly discovered how much "bigger" God was than I had ever imagined.

I was incapable of understanding basic attributes of God. What could a neglected child know about joy? How can someone with patterns of withdrawal know anything about peace? My concept of love had been distorted beyond recognition. And to be told that Christians should exhibit the fruit of the Holy Spirit—love, joy, peace, patience, kindness, goodness, faithfulness, gentleness, and self-control (see Galatians 5:22-23)—was purely an intellectual lesson and had nothing to do, in my case, with experience.

But when I finally got to the point where my strongholds were causing more pain than I thought I could endure, God showed me more clearly who he *really* was. He gave me the weapons I needed to demolish my strongholds. And with those strongholds behind me, my pain was replaced with all those wonderful characteristics I had heard about but never experienced.

My concept of God never came close to being an "understanding" of him. It still doesn't. The "bigness" of God is beyond anything we can ever envision with our human minds. At one time, that might have been a frightening thought for me. But now, in the context of his love and freedom, it is a glorious surprise. I can spend the rest of my life getting to know God better—strengthening the relationship and seeing more and more of what he is like. And no matter how much I discover, there is still an enormous amount yet to be known. Since finding freedom from my strongholds, every day with God contains new surprises.

Surprise 3: Salvation is sufficient. I had a limited concept of evil. I had a limited concept of God. I also had a limited concept of salvation. This was really a surprise for me.

So many times I think people consider salvation as an event. "Jesus saves." That's it. Believe in him and escape hell. Then it's over and done with.

I agree that salvation *is* an event in one sense. Faith in Jesus certainly does have saving power, and Christ's forgiveness is once and for all. He doesn't forgive us and then change his mind. He doesn't regenerate us and then de-generate us. Yet I've come to see that salvation is also a *process*.

I believe the initial act (event) of salvation begins the process. But too many of us stop there. Peter tells us: "Like newborn babies, crave pure spiritual milk, so that by it you may grow up in your salvation, now that you have tasted that the Lord is good" (1 Pt 2:2-3). He seems to suggest that our initial forgiveness of sin is just a "taste" of what salvation can be.

And in chapter one we saw that Paul tells us to "continue to work out your salvation with fear and trembling" (Phil 2:12). If salvation means little more than "fire insurance" for us, we miss out on a lot of what God has to offer us.

After getting past my personal strongholds and at last being able to evaluate my life from a more objective viewpoint, I could see the far-reaching effects of salvation. Yes, God certainly saved me from hell and forgave my sins, for which I will be eternally grateful. But his salvation then extended to other areas of my life. He saved me from the evil that had been controlling my life. He saved me from the despair and worthlessness I was feeling. He saved me from spiritual apathy. And his salvation continues to lift me above the situations of life that previously would have had much more control or negative influence on me.

None of these things are automatic. I do have to "work out" my salvation in most cases—putting into practice the truth of God's Word and keeping my relationship with him strong. But the surprises of salvation continue. I echo the words of the author of Hebrews who reminds us that we have "such a great salvation" (Heb 2:3).

It makes sense that I would be so surprised about the extent of salvation. Since I previously did not have an adequate understanding of the nature of evil, I couldn't possibly appreciate God's salvation as I should. But as I began to see evil more clearly, I also saw more clearly who God is and what his plan of salvation means in my life. And I discovered these wonderful surprises that continue to inspire me. I hope they help you as well.

DAY BY DAY, AND WITH EACH PASSING MOMENT

Earlier in the book I compared strongholds to cancer—particularly in regard to their tendency to spread. Perhaps you know someone who has won a battle with cancer. If so, you will probably witness a significant change in the habits of that person. Even discovery of a "minor" skin cancer can jolt a person into a significant change of lifestyle. After the cancer is removed, you'll probably notice that the person stops lying out in the sun. He or she may not even leave the house on a sunny day without suntan lotion and a hat. The person usually becomes more vocal in sharing his or her experiences with friends, hoping they will avoid the same results. And perhaps a scar from surgery will remain to remind the person of a "near miss" with disaster.

After battling your strongholds, you may have a few scars. But scars don't hurt. They are reminders of pain, but it's pain that was *in the past.* We are now able to make wise decisions based on past experiences, and to share those experiences with others.

This book has been my attempt to share my own experiences with you. But even though you're at the end of this book, you're only at the beginning of your search for freedom. I hope that by now you're looking back at the ruins of all the strongholds of your past. I hope that you are closer to God right now than you've ever been before in your life. And frankly, I hope you're feeling a little bit scared, because that's almost always a sure sign that you've truly broken free of the destructive patterns of your past.

Perhaps you haven't accomplished all I've said is possible. If not, you might need to go back to the sections of this book that were most difficult for you to understand or agree with. I realize that freedom and forgiveness will come much harder for some people than others. But I am convinced beyond a doubt that such things are possible for everyone. If you still need to work on some strongholds, I urge you not to give up now.

Let us not become weary in doing good,
for at the proper time we will reap a harvest
if we do not give up.
Galatians 6:9

If you are experiencing freedom for the first time in years—perhaps for the first time ever—bask in the feeling for a while. Get used to it. Take some time to savor the new experience. Breathe deeply of the sweet, free air. Then begin to prepare yourself. It won't be long before familiar people or situations show up that will threaten to take that freedom away from you.

But you'll notice that you're stronger now than you used to be.

You still have those weapons God provides that have "divine power to demolish strongholds." Nobody can ever enslave you again... not without your permission. So don't let that happen.

I'll be praying for you, as I pray for all the readers of my books and the hurting people who come to Rapha for help. We're all in this struggle together. After you get past your strongholds, I encourage you to make yourself available to help someone else.

I'll close with a challenge for all of us: "Let us not become weary in doing good, for at the proper time we will reap a harvest if we do not give up" (Gal 6:9).

The search for freedom continues. The harvest is ahead of you. Just don't give up.

The Spirit of the Lord God is upon me, because the Lord has anointed me to bring good news to the afflicted; He has sent me to bind up the brokenhearted, to proclaim liberty to captives, and freedom to prisoners; to proclaim the favorable year of the Lord.

Isaiah 61:1-2, NAS

Questions for Small Group Study

Chapter 1—How Freedom Is Lost

Objective: To see the pervasiveness of sin in our lives.

1. Open a newspaper or tune in to today's news. Note the headlines and top stories. What do these things tell you about the depravity of humankind?

2. How does the sin of the world affect you and your family?

3. What areas of your own life resemble the problem areas you can detect in the lives of others?

4. As a child of God, how do you feel when you give in to the temptations of the world?

Chapter 2—Stuck with Childhood Patterns
Objective: To understand how we are
held captive by childhood patterns.

1. Have you ever been addicted to something—drugs, alcohol, cigarettes, chewing tobacco, caffeine, chocolate? Did you try to "kick the habit"? Did you ever relapse? Explain the difficulties you faced while trying to stop using these substances.

2. How do you respond to crises?

3. How do you respond to situations that do not turn out like you had expected?

4. In what ways do your responses make you feel like a prisoner?

Chapter 3—Childhood Behaviors
Objective: To identify specific childish behavior
that continues to affect us.

1. Share stories about yourself or other people you know who display the following types of behavior as adults:

- Throwing temper tantrums

- Using crying to get what they want

- Whining

- Clinging

- Bickering

- Being strong-willed

- Being the center of attention

- Being irresponsible

2. What do you suppose adults are thinking when they act in childish ways?

3. How does your own thinking sometimes resemble that of a child?

Chapter 4—Emotions of Childhood
Objective: To see why some people never seem to "grow up," and to identify specific fears that may influence personal decisions and growth.

1. Use the "How Do You Feel?" chart to describe your emotional state right now.

2. Which of the four false beliefs would you say has most affected you in the past:

   - I must meet certain standards in order to feel good about myself.

   - I must be approved (accepted) by certain other people in order to feel good about myself.

   - Those who fail are unworthy of love and deserve to be punished.

   - I am what I am. I cannot change. I am hopeless.

3. In what ways do you experience:

   - The fear of failure?

   - The fear of rejection?

   - The fear of punishment?

   - The fear of feeling shame and other negative emotions?

4. What was your greatest fear as a child? What is your greatest fear today? Do you find it easier to give in to fear, or to combat it? Why?

Chapter 5—Understanding the Enemy Within

Objective: To identify and discuss "fight" and "flight" responses to emotional pain.

1. What is the most painful event you can recall as a child? How did you respond to it when it occurred?

2. How do you still use methods of "fight" or "flight" to avoid pain?

3. How do you suppose your current behaviors are connected to your childhood ones?

Chapter 6—A Closer Look at Strongholds

Objective: To define, discuss, and begin to identify specific strongholds.

1. Based on your personal experience, how would *you* define a stronghold?

2. Determine how strongly you feel you are influenced by each of the following categories of strongholds. Number them from 1 (what you feel strongest) to 11 (what you feel least).

   _ Depression   _ Doubt
   _ Bitterness   _ Rebellion
   _ Insecurity   _ Pride
   _ Infirmities and addictions   _ Sexual impurity
   _ Deceit   _ Occult
   _ Fears

3. How do you think your life would be different if the things you marked as "1," "2," and "3" were no longer problems for you?

Chapter 7—Messages from the Past; Help for the Present

Objective: To see how the power of the Holy Spirit can begin to counteract the negative messages we have absorbed during our lifetimes.

1. Review the "labels" and "looks" you checked at the end of the chapter. Think back to your most recent experience in each case. How do these messages continue to affect you?

2. In the space below, write down a list of "labels" or "looks" that you communicated to someone else in the last thirty days. If you repeated the same message more than once, circle it.

3. Ask God to help you be completely honest. Then repeat question 2.

4. What do your answers suggest about patterns of responses in your life?

Chapter 8—Getting to the Root of the Problem

Objective: To identify the connections between emotional pain, bitterness, and unforgiveness.

1. Think of situations in your life where you have refused to forgive someone for a lengthy period of time. In each case, how was bitterness at the "root" of your unforgiveness? Why did you feel bitter?

2. When was the last time you can recall using a "fight" response to a problem? What, specifically, did you do? Why?

3. When was the last time you can recall responding to a problem with a "flight" instinct? What were the circumstances? Why did you try to flee the problem?

Chapter 9—Hearing God's Voice
Objective: To examine the many different ways that God might choose to communicate with humankind.

1. How many different ways can you think of that God communicated with biblical characters? Think about Moses, Daniel, Elijah, and Balaam, for example.

2. How does God communicate today?

3. Describe how God has communicated to you using any of the following methods that apply:

   • Through the Bible

   • Through the Holy Spirit

   • Audibly

   • Confirming his presence in your life through feelings of peace

   • Other:

4. Pray that God will show you how to "hear" him much more clearly from now on.

Chapter 10—Prayer Paves the Way

Objective: To see the importance of prayer when
preparing to demolish strongholds.

1. On a scale of 1 (least) to 10 (most), how important would you say prayer is in your life?

2. If God acted in your life only in response to prayer, do you think you would pray more often? Why or why not?

3. Look through the chapter and write down the three things you think are most important to remember about prayer.

Chapter 11—The Path to Freedom

Objective: To discover and begin to apply the CROP
process for destroying strongholds.

1. Think of an offense against you which has caused some pain but has not consumed you. Then:

   • Describe the event.

   • Describe what you were thinking when it happened.

- Explain what you expected to happen.

- Tell how it affected the way you felt.

- Explain how you responded, and why.

2. Experience the CROP process:

- Confession: Determine what stronghold, patterns, or sin is obviously present. Confess this to God.
- Repentance: How can you turn away from your wrong responses?

- Obedience: What actions do you need to take?

- Praise: How can you thank God specifically for his help and presence?

Chapter 12—Avoiding Common Failures and Setbacks
Objective: To identify potential pitfalls with the CROP process, and avoid them.

1. What strongholds or patterns keep you from experiencing all that God has for you and from enjoying peace and freedom?

2. What areas of your life still require forgiveness?

3. Which of the steps in the CROP process is most difficult for you right now? Why?

4. Ask God to provide all the strength and courage you need to keep moving ahead with your life.

About Rapha

Rapha was founded in 1986 by Robert S. McGee. As an outpatient Christian counselor, McGee was frustrated with the lack of quality, biblically-based Christian impatient care available where he could refer his clients. He founded Rapha to meet that need. The name Rapha is Hebrew for "Our God Who Heals." Since its inception, Rapha has been used of God to treat thousands of individuals across the country.

Rapha's mission is to assist those suffering from emotional, relational and substance abuse problems in the healing process from a distinctive, biblically-based, Christ-centered approach. Today, Rapha is one of the nation's largest managers of psychiatric and substance abuse treatment from a distinctively Christian perspective. In hospitals and treatment centers located nationwide, Rapha offers a continuum of care for adults and adolescents including acute inpatient, sub-acute, residential and partial hospitalization; day, evening, and weekend programs; intensive outpatient; and outpatient network; conferences; support group training; books and materials.

WHAT MAKES RAPHA DIFFERENT?

"Since our inception in 1986 we are still asked 'what makes you different?' The following characteristics will show you why Rapha is distinctive in its field:

- Rapha is managed by a team comprised of healthcare professionals who are committed Christians.

- We view treatment as a triad, and thus our physicians, nursing personnel, and therapy staff are each equally responsible for patient care. They are highly qualified, licensed or certified professionals who are committed to a Christian-based treatment model.

- Our program is unique. The three elements which are common denominators in our treatment approach are:

  1. *Focus on the identity of God.* This includes modification of our perceptions of who God is, understanding how we relate to him and improving our communication with the Lord.
  2. *Clarification of self-identity.* This is based upon understanding and experiencing our self-worth according to who God says we are as his children, as opposed to who we think we are based on our performance and others' opinions. This also leads us to a healthy acceptance of responsibility for our own actions.
  3. *Processing of forgiveness.* This includes forgiveness of self, others, and God, and dealing with offenses, unforgiveness, and strongholds. We assist those who are struggling with unhealthy behavioral patterns in breaking the bondage and finding freedom. The experience of forgiveness is the change agent which separates Christianity from all other religions. Our clinical expertise and sound biblical principles make Rapha a one-of-a-kind alternative."

—Don Sapaugh, CEO, Rapha

If you or someone you know needs help with an emotional or substance abuse problem, call Rapha today at 1-800-383-HOPE.

Another Book of Interest
by the Author of
The Search for Freedom

Father Hunger
Robert S. McGee

"Father hunger" describes the emptiness that many of us experience because we still crave the comfort and security that our fathers did not provide for us.

Your relationship with your father not only affects your emotional style, your relationships with your children and your spouse, and your ability to handle life in general, but it deeply affects the way you think about God. Here is a book for men and women who hunger for something deeper and more authentic in their relationships with their fathers. **$12.99**